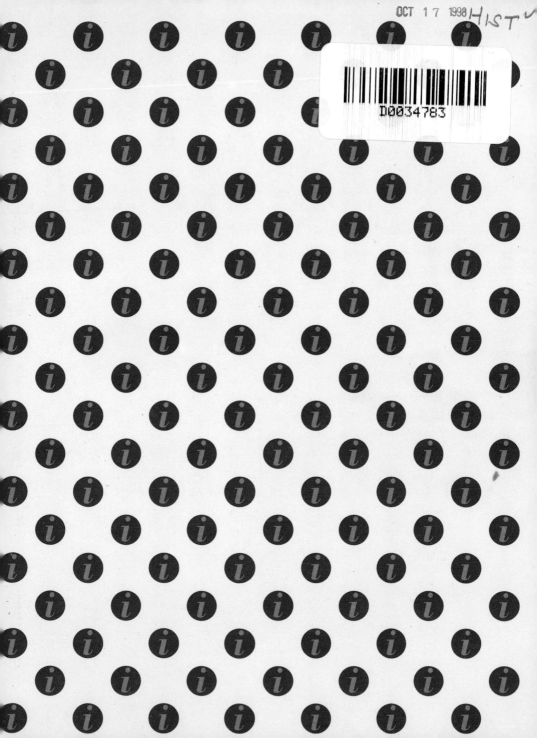

# TARTANS

The new compact study guide and identifier

# IDENTIFYING

# TARTANS

The new compact study guide and identifier

## Edited by Blair Urquhart

CHARTWELL
BOOKS, INC.

A QUINTET BOOK

Published by Chartwell Books
A Division of Book Sales, Inc.
110 Enterprise Avenue
Secaucus, New Jersey 07094

ISBN 0-7858-0050-6

This book was designed and produced by
Quintet Publishing Limited
6 Blundell Street
London N7 9BH

Creative Director: Richard Dewing
Designer: Wayne Blades
Project Editor: Helen Denholm
Editor: Lydia Darbyshire
Photographer: Blair Urquhart

ACKNOWLEDGEMENTS
The text and illustrations in the Tartans Directory are the copyright of
the Scottish Tartans Society. In the case of a small number of modern
tartans, the copyright of the design still belongs to the designer or
promoter.

The publisher and editor would like to thank the following Fellows of
the Scottish Tartans Society whose original research has contributed
greatly to this guide: Captain T. Stuart Davidson, Dr. Micheil
MacDonald, Ruairidh MacLeod, Angela Nisbet, Sylvia Slater and
Dr. Gordon Teall of Teallach. Thanks is also due to Keith and
Elizabeth Lumsden who maintain the Society's archives. Additional
samples of tartan were provided by Lochcarron of Scotland, MacAlister
of Glenbarr, Capt. Stuart MacBride, Mr Derek Young and Mrs Annette
Brown. Thanks are also due to Maggie MacDonald, archivist at Clan
Donald Lands Trust; Dr Colin Roth; Mr Euan Hunter Smith; the
Mitchell Library, Glasgow.

Typeset in Great Britain by
Central Southern Typesetters, Eastbourne
Manufactured in Singapore by
Eray Scan Pte Ltd
Printed in Singapore by Star Standard Pte Ltd

# CONTENTS

# FOREWORD

"**B**RING FORRIT THE TARTAN" was the motto chosen for the Scottish Tartans Society by the late Sir Iain Moncreiffe of that Ilk. Bringing forward the tartan for the enjoyment of the reader is what the Editor has achieved in this guide.

Tartans have always formed part of Scotland's historic heritage and it is a compliment to their country of origin that they have become so widespread throughout the English and Gaelic speaking world. They are probably more popular now than they have ever been because they have come to symbolize the spirit of families, clans and districts and, more recently, corporate institutions.

This guide outlines the history of tartan and illustrates some of the well known designs which are to be seen today. For those who enjoy tartan spotting it will be of invaluable assistance.

Since the Scottish Tartans Society was formally inaugurated in 1963 by the late Sir Thomas Innes of Learney, Lord Lyon King of Arms, 1945–69, it has become widely recognized as the principal authority on tartans and Highland dress. The dedicated endeavours of the scholars and fellows of the Society have led to the establishment of one of the finest collections of material in this field of study in the world. Their research has culminated in the establishment of the Register of All Publicly Known Tartans which contains details of more than 2,000 tartans and which is constantly being updated.

The authenticity of this guide has been assured by the Editor having unrestricted access to the comprehensive archives of the Scottish Tartans Society at its headquarters in Pitlochry, Perthshire, Scotland. The Tartans Directory comprises copyright extracts from the Register of All Publicly Known Tartans and includes a representative selection of tartans associated with families and clans.

The Scottish Tartans Society seeks to encourage excellence in all matters relating to tartan and Highland dress. The highly esteemed Fellowship may be awarded to scholars who publish the results of advanced research into their subject. In order that the public may have an insight into its research work, the Society maintains Museums in Scotland and in the USA.

In recognition of its contribution towards the preservation of Scotland's cultural tradition, the Lord Lyon, King of Arms, has conferred upon the Scottish Tartans Society the special status of an "Incorporation Noble in the Noblesse of Scotland".

May you, the reader, find pleasure in sharing Scotland's unique heritage of Tartan and Highland dress.

Dr D. Gordon Teall of Teallach
The Executive President of the Scottish Tartans Society

# THE ORIGINS OF
# CLAN TARTANS

It is now generally accepted that clan tartans were established and named towards the end of the 18th century. Prior to that time, while clans, districts and tartans were often closely associated, the idea of a single uniform clan tartan had not yet emerged. It would be wrong, however, to assume that the tartan patterns were created at this time. William Wilson, the foremost weaving manufacturer since around 1770, took a great interest in reproducing "perfectly genuine patterns" and engaged in extensive correspondence with his Highland agents to gather information and actual samples of the cloth woven in the clan districts.

At that time the natural development of the art of tartan manufacture in the Highlands had been completely curtailed for over 50 years. The battle of Culloden (1746) was still within living memory and the disarming acts which followed included the proscription of Highland dress which was not repealed until 1782. Tartan manufacture survived only in the hands of the military and their Lowland suppliers. Efforts to restore the spirit and culture of the Highlands after this lengthy period of repression were encouraged by the newly formed Highland Societies in London

(1778) and Edinburgh (1780). The warlike reputation of tartan, ruthlessly crushed at home, was put to great military advantage by the Highland regiments in their exploits abroad. By 1822, the year of the first royal visit to Scotland since the rebellion, all the ingredients for a spectacular tartan revival were in place. Wilson had recorded over 200 setts in his firm's pattern books,

*A print by Robert Ranald McIan of a figure in the MacAuley Clan tartan, 1845.*

many of them tentatively named, and the Highland Society of London had persuaded the majority of the clan chiefs to account for their clan tartans. Due to the efforts of Sir Walter Scott, the royal seal of approval was added to the now highly fashionable Highland costume by a kilted King George IV. The chiefs of the clans were commanded to attend the King at Holyrood Palace in Edinburgh wearing their Highland dress. This royal patronage was continued and extended by Queen Victoria in her passion for things Scottish.

Evidence of the previous existence of tartan dates back to the 3rd century AD. A small sample of woollen check cloth dating from that period was found buried close to the Roman Antonine Wall near Falkirk. It had been used as a stopper in an earthenware pot to protect a treasure trove of silver coins. This is known as the Falkirk sett. The two colours of the sample were identified as the undyed brown and white of the native Soay Sheep.

References to tartans occur in various historic documents, paintings and illustrations. A charter granted to Hector MacLean of Duart in 1587 for lands in Islay details a feu duty payable in the form of 60 ells of cloth of white, black and green colours (the colours of Hunting MacLean of Duart tartan), and an eyewitness account of the battle of Killiecrankie in 1689 describes "McDonells men in their triple stripes".

It is reasonable to assume that any tightly knit community would wear the cloth produced by the local weaver in quantities that would limit the variety of patterns, and that when they went to war, many would be dressed in the same material.

Many references support the role of the chief in deciding the pattern and the colour of the plaids to be worn in battle. This tradition is maintained to the present day. New tartans accredited by the Scottish Tartans Society must have the approval of the chief (see MacLeod Red, page 60) or head of the family (see MacBride, page 49) if they are to be known by his name. In some cases (see Young, page 78) the authority of the clan society is recognized.

*The Buchanan Clan tartan.*

# ~ TARTAN TIMECHART ~

**Pre-1000 AD** The Falkirk sett dating from Roman times.

**c.1093** The Magnus Barefoot saga refers to "... short kyrtles and upper garments ..."

**c.1100** The de Moravia tribe includes both Murrays and Sutherlands, later separated geographically, but retaining similar tartans.

**1266** Western Isles annexed to the Crown of Scotland.

**1314** Battle of Bannockburn between Robert the Bruce of Scotland and King Edward II of England.

**1468** Orkney and Shetland acquired from Norway.

**1538** King James V's treasurers account for "Heland tartane".

**1540** King James V visits the Western Isles.

**1548** "... wool of many colours ..." mentioned in account of the siege of Haddington.

**1560** The Reformation of the Church. Catholic/Protestant division.

**1572** Supposed date of the original *Vestiarium Scoticum.*

**1587** Hector MacLean's feus are paid in tartan cloth of white, black and green, the colours of the Hunting MacLean tartan.

**1603** Union of the Crowns of Scotland and England.

**1618** Sir Robert Gordon asks for the red and white stripes to be removed from the plaids of the men to bring their dress into harmony with the other septs.

**1692** The Massacre of the MacIans of Glencoe by government forces.

**1703** Martin Martin's *Description of the Western Islands of Scotland* relates tartan patterns to the "place of residence" of the wearer.

**1715** The first Jacobite rising. The battle of Sheriffmuir.

**1721** Sir Richard Urquhart allegedly copies the original *Vestiarium Scoticum* into a document known as the Cromarty Manuscript.

**1721** The "Christina Young" blanket. An early example of homespun handloom weaving preserved at the Scottish Tartans Museum.

**1725** General Wade made Commander in Chief of the Highland Companies.

**1739** Black Watch tartan issued to the Highland Regiments.

**1745** The third Jacobite rising.

**1746** Highland Dress proscribed.

**1759** Birth of Robert Burns (d.1796).

**1770** William Wilson & Sons supply military tartans.

**1775** Acts against Clan Gregor repealed.

**1782** The acts against Highland dress repealed.

**1797** Napoleonic Wars. Homeguard formed as "fencible regiments" often wearing the tartan of their commander.

**1810–20** General Cockburn collects tartans.

**1815** Highland Society of London resolves to collect clan tartans.

**1819** Wilson's of Bannockburn produce their first pattern book, details of which have become known only in the last 30 years.

**1822** Sir Walter Scott stage-manages the visit of King George IV to Edinburgh. Great tartan fashion revival.

**1826** Logan begins research on his book, *The Scottish Gael,* which contains the first published list of named clan tartans (1831).

**1829** Self-styled "Sobieski Stuart" brothers begin work on the *Vestiarium Scoticum,* published in 1842.

**1963** Formation of the Scottish Tartans Society, inaugurated by the Lord Lyon.

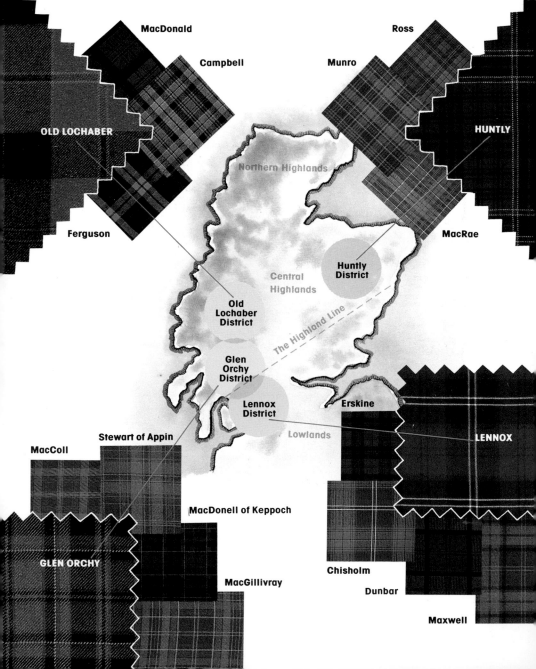

# ~ DISTRICT ORIGINS OF CLAN TARTANS ~

MacDonald

Campbell

Ross

Munro

OLD LOCHABER

HUNTLY

Ferguson

MacRae

Northern Highlands

Huntly
District

Central
Highlands

Old
Lochaber
District

The Highland Line

Glen
Orchy
District

Lennox
District

Erskine

LENNOX

Lowlands

MacColl

Stewart of Appin

GLEN ORCHY

MacDonell of Keppoch

Chisholm

MacGillivray

Dunbar

Maxwell

# THE DISTRICT
# ORIGINS OF CLAN TARTANS

Many of the oldest clan tartans may have originated in the work of local weavers, whose designs became the patterns we now know as district tartans.

## THE HUNTLY

Records of the Huntly district tartan can be traced to the early 18th century when it was worn by Gordons, Forbes, Brodies and Munros in the eastern part of the Central Highlands. Only the Munro tartan still retains elements of the Huntly design but there is a strong resemblance to the Ross and the MacRae tartans as they are today and these clans from the west may have adopted the design to show their Jacobite sympathies. An example known as "The Prince's Own", a MacRae tartan, is known to have been worn by Prince Charles Edward at the start of the '45 campaign.

## THE OLD LOCHABER

The Old Lochaber may have provided the basis for the tartans of the Campbells and the MacDonalds. The green, black and blue is typical of many west coast patterns, including the four main Campbell tartans, and was adopted by the military as the Black Watch. The MacDonalds placed greater emphasis on the red in their clan sett. The Fergusons, who lived in the heart of the Lochaber district, have a tartan that clearly derives from that area.

## THE GLEN ORCHY

The Glen Orchy district tartan provides the pattern structure that is repeated in clan setts in the Central Highlands in both green and red tartans. The structure is made up of boxes within boxes, with the dark squares alternating with the open squares of the ground colour. The clans which adopted this style include the Stewarts of Appin, the MacColls, the MacDonalds of Keppoch, the MacGillivrays and the MacIntyres.

## THE LENNOX

Lennox, near Glasgow, lies on the Highland Line, that geological boundary that separates the Highlander from the Lowlander. The tartan was discovered in a copy of an old portrait of the Countess of Lennox dating from the 16th century, with evidence to support its district connections. It is included here because of its similarity to many Lowland tartans which first appeared in the *Vestiarium Scoticum*. The Sobieski Stuarts claimed that their work was based on an authentic 16th century manuscript but later research has shown it to be, at best, a mixture of fact and fiction. Whatever the case, there is no doubt that the Erskines, the Maxwells, the Lindsays, the Cunninghams, the Chisholms and the Wallaces, to name but a few, have a tartan with a design which has developed from district origins.

# USING THIS GUIDE

For each tartan information is given on the name, the earliest known date, the earliest recorded sources, the status and type, as well as specific information on the tartan's history and details of its clan and family associations.

## THE NAME

The present-day name of the tartan is given, along with several descriptive terms which have acquired special meanings in this context. Strong feelings surround the use of the word "clan". Some would insist that only the acknowledged Highland tribes can be so described, while others regard it as a synonym for family or, in fact, any group of people acting with a common interest. In this

*A figure in the Buchanan Clan tartan by McIan, 1845.*

book both Highland and Lowland families are described as clans, in line with the many historical references which use the term. Tartans of branches of the main clans are also described as clan tartans. Some names are associated with more than one clan, and it is appropriate in these instances to refer to the family tartan.

Hunting tartans are designed in subdued colours, often greens or blues, to blend with the natural environment. Wearing of these tartans is not restricted to the grouse moors, but is intended for everyday use and informal occasions. Some clans wear the Black Watch as their hunting sett, like the Munros.

Dress tartans are designed by altering one of the background colours of the formal sett to white. Kilts made of this material are usually worn for dancing; not to be confused with "formal dress" or "evening dress".

Names which include Mac, Mc or M' are always spelt Mac in full, followed by a capital letter, except where the name refers to an individual who has stated a preference by spelling his name in some other way. In Gaelic, Mac and the name are two separate words.

## EARLIEST KNOWN DATE

This entry records the first reference to the tartan under its present name. The thread count at that time may be different from the illustrated sett, but there will be sufficient similarity to suggest that the main elements of the design are still apparent in the modern version. The use of parentheses indicates that there is a degree of doubt about the historical validity of the reference.

## EARLIEST KNOWN SOURCE

This refers to the first source of information on the exact sett described. A visit to the Queen Street Museum in Edinburgh or the Mitchell Library in Glasgow will reward the investigator with a glimpse of the subtle beauty of these early samples. In some cases the earliest source will be the designer, but more often it will be one of the early collections or publications. If the pattern has altered since the earliest date, the source reference will have a later date. The main sources are listed in the next section of the book.

## STATUS

The tartan of a Highland clan is determined by the clan chief. The clansmen and followers (blood relations and families taking protection from the clan) wear the tartan of the chief. In most cases the sett has been acknowledged for generations and is well known to chief and clansmen alike, but occasionally the chief may pronounce on a new pattern or disassociate himself from an old one. A case in point is the Clan Campbell tartan. The present chief does not acknowledge the well-known Campbell of Argyll, and instead prefers to wear the plain Black Watch Campbell in ancient colours.

The Highland Society of London has a collection of tartans in which each sample is "certified by the chief" and bears his seal and signature. The Lord Lyon maintains the Lyon Court Books and the Public Register of All Arms and Bearings, in which are registered those clan and family tartans appearing in the families' coats of arms, usually as the background to the clan badge.

The Scottish Tartans Society awards an Accreditation status to newly designed tartans, including clan, family, district, regimental, corporate and clan society tartans, in the Register of All Publicly Known Tartans. Acknowledged tartans that do not fall into any of these categories are listed as Recorded in this register.

*The Scottish Tartans Museum in Comrie, Perthshire.*

## TYPE

There are three types of pattern. **Symmetrical setts** contain two pivots – the points where the sequence of stripes, starting at the pivot, can be seen to be identical in four directions: north, south, east and west. The two pivots are connected along the diagonal by plain squares each of a single colour. The full sett is the sequence of colours read from right to left, turned about the pivot, and repeated left to right. It is usually between 5 and 7 inches (13 and 18 cm) in width to accommodate the kilting (pleats). A symmetrical tartan can be recorded as a half sett.

**Asymmetrical setts** have no true pivots although they can sometimes appear to. The pattern is repeated from right to left across the width of the cloth. Manufacturers using double-width looms may change the direction of the pattern at the centre, where the cloth will be folded, to allow tailors to match the colours when cutting items of clothing other than kilts. Tailors' off-cuts can contain some pieces easily mistaken for examples of a symmetrical form of an asymmetrical tartan. The full sett must be recorded, beginning at the colour whose first letter is nearest to the beginning of the alphabet. It is also necessary to establish the front of the cloth: the side on which the twill effect appears to make diagonal lines from bottom left to top right. The knots on manufactured cloth are always pulled to the back.

**Equal check** is the simplest tartan, involving only two colours. The MacGregor tartan known as Rob Roy is an example and is a black and red check. The Moncreiffe is a red and green equal check.

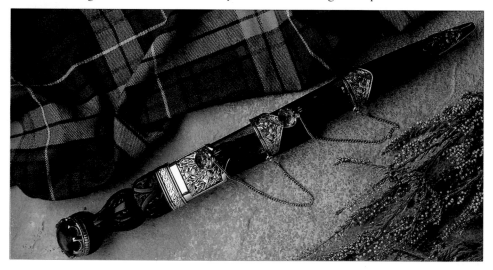

*A sgian-dhu; a short sword with a knife and fork attached to the sheath.*

# SOURCES OF THE
# EARLIEST TARTANS

## WILSON OF BANNOCKBURN

William Wilson & Sons came into being as commercial weavers about 1770 in the historic village of Bannockburn near Stirling. Initially, the firm's main task was to supply tartan cloth for the military, which was engaged at that time in keeping the peace north of the Highland Line (a geological boundary separating the Highlands from the Lowlands), and enforcing the ban on the wearing of tartan that had been imposed by the Act of Proscription, 1746. The landed gentry and the army were exempted for this restriction, as were women, and Wilson had a virtual monopoly of the trade.

Many items of correspondence relating to the business have been preserved over the years, but detailed study of the historical evidence is comparatively recent. The most important sources for the tartans in use today are the firm's pattern books of 1819 and 1847, which give precise details of colours and threads.

Another interesting facet of the firm's papers is the emergence of names to describe the various patterns. Under the pressure of demand, Wilson encouraged his agents (salesmen) to search for the "true" designs produced in small quanti-ties by handloom weavers throughout the Highlands. The clan names associated with tartans today were very much in their infancy. For example, the Baillie tartan was described in 1797 as "the sett that the Baillie Fencibles wear". Most of the patterns were simply numbered and occasionally had a name tagged on for additional reference. MacNab, for example, reads "No. 199 or MacNab"; MacLachlan (now Moncreiffe) reads "No. 99 or Small MacLachlan".

## LOGAN

James Logan spent five years researching for his book *The Scottish Gael or Celtic Manners, as Preserved among the Highlanders* (1831). He asked for, and received, the assistance of the Highland Society of London to provide an appendix of tartans at the end of the book. Logan had to choose between the certified tartans of the chiefs from the Highland Society and the more commercially orientated findings of William Wilson. Logan had asked Wilson to send him "patterns of all the clan and family tartans". Wilson's list includes such comments as "McDougal – 1 set & part – as we make it" or "McKintosh – Chisholm no white, ditto, shewy pattern with yellow".

Clan name tartans were very much in demand by the time Logan published his work in 1831. Of the 55 tartans published, 33 are directly attributable to the Highland Society. Only five came solely from Wilson's pattern books, although many appeared in both and sometimes, rather confusingly, with different names. Of Logan's patterns, 10 came from other sources, which he did not reveal. Logan himself had been on the tartan trail, "wandering through Scotland collecting information of antiquarian interest". Apart from some well-documented mistakes, Logan's work is now considered the most authoritative early source for Highland clan tartans.

## COCKBURN COLLECTION

The Cockburn Collection, which is housed is the Mitchell Library in Glasgow, was put together by General Sir William Cockburn between 1810 and 1820. Labels, where they exist, are pinned on the cloth in Cockburn's own handwriting and dated 1815. Most of the samples are believed to have been manufactured by William Wilson of Bannockburn, but their special interest lies in the fact that the precise details of colour and threads can be compared with the manufacturer's pattern books, which were compiled in 1819. The collection has 56 specimens of very fine, hard tartan mounted in a single, double-folio volume. The brightly coloured over-checks are often woven in a slightly heavier silk yarn.

The Collection has been annotated in pencil with comparisons to the *Vestiarium Scoticum*. The author of these notes, which are dated 1930, clearly believed the *Vestiarium* to be the greater authority, and perhaps underestimated the historic value of the Collection, which is now regarded as one of the earliest tartan collections of known provenance.

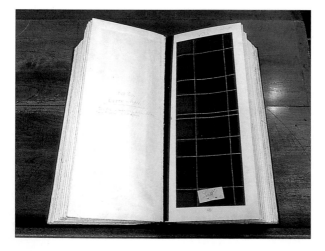

*The Hay and Leith tartan sample from the Cockburn Collection.*

## THE HIGHLAND SOCIETY OF LONDON

As early as 1815 the committee of the Highland Society of London was convinced of the existence of "named Highland clan tartans" and resolved to commission the preparation of a comprehensive collection. It proposed to request all the clans to submit an authentic sample, which would be signed and sealed by the chief or head of the family. The effects of this decision were far-reaching. Many of the chiefs were unaware of what, exactly, constituted a clan tartan, but they were anxious to comply with the request of such an august body as the Highland Society. Lord Macdonald's reply (on page 18) illustrates the position. By 1816 at least 74 specimens had been found. Correspondence dated 3 February 1826 reveals that 34 authenticated pieces were still intact and that "about forty other pieces in the (deal) box, on some of which the seals were not legible, were unauthenticated". Many of the pieces were damaged by moths. M. S. Metcalf, clerk to the Society at the time, went on to suggest that "a piece be cut from each of the certified tartans and pasted in a book ... to preserve the pattern". Fortunately, the off-cuts were also preserved so that the chiefs' seals can still be matched to tartans they certified. The collection and certification of tartans has continued to this day, but although the Collection was recently catalogued, no detailed analysis has ever been published.

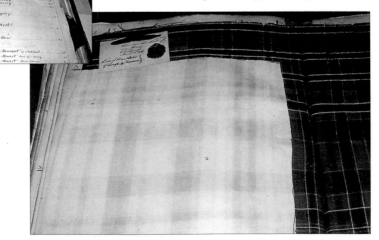

*The Index of Certified Tartans from the Highland Society of London.*

*The remains of a sample of the MacAlister Clan tartan from the Highland Society.*

## – LORD MACDONALD'S REPLY TO THE –
## – HIGHLAND SOCIETY –

October 1st, 1815

Dear Sir,

. . . A Resolution of The Highland Society of London has just been transmitted to me, and as it
Appears to be the Anxious Wish of the Society to collect Patterns duly Authenticated of all the
different Tartans, They have requested that I should forward Mine When I may find it
Convenient. I now send You a Copy of the Resolution.

"At a General Meeting of The Highland Society of London held on Saturday The 8th of
April 1815 His Royal Highness The Duke of Kent and Strathearn in the Chair – Resolved
That Lord Macdonald be respectfully Solicited to furnish the Society with as Much of the
Tartan of his Lordships Clan as will serve to Show the Pattern and to Authenticate the
Same by Attaching Thereunto a Card bearing the Impression of His Lordship's Arms.
Edward by his Royal Highness The Duke of Kent and Strathearn.
James Hamilton Secretary."

Being really ignorant of what is exactly The Macdonald Tartan, I request you will have the
goodness to exert every Means in your power to Obtain a perfectly genuine Pattern, Such as Will
Warrant me in Authenticating it with my Arms. Perhaps Sir John Murray May be able to put you
in The Way of gaining Some information. I request that you will pay immediately into the hands
of Mr Lewis Gordon The Secretary of The Highland Society of Edin. The Sum of Twenty Guineas
as My Contribution for defraying the expenses of the Compilation and Publication of a Scoto-
Gaelic Dictionary.
I remain Dr Sir
most faithfully Your's
Macdonald

## VESTIARIUM SCOTICUM

This remarkable book was produced between 1829 and 1842, when it was finally published. The authors, John Sobieski Stolberg Stuart Hay and his younger brother, Charles Edward, claimed that their father was the legitimate son of Prince Charles Edward Stuart by his wife, Princess Louisa of Stolberg Gedern. They put about a story that they had in their possession of manuscript based on a 16th-century publication held by their father and acquired from the Scots College of Douai in France. This document, the Cromarty Manuscript, was said to have been written by Sir Richard Urquhart around 1721.

This imaginative fabrication gained the Sobieski brothers admittance to the social circles of the Scottish gentry in London and the company of the chiefs in Scotland, many of whom were as lacking in knowledge of their "official" clan tartan as their guests.

The "new" patterns were well researched, and convincing historical connections can be found in the designs; a procedure often adopted in the creation of new designs in the present day. The most fundamental deception, however, was in the creation of Lowland tartans, for as Sir Walter Scott observed: "The general proposition that the Lowlanders ever wore plaids is difficult to swallow." Nevertheless, many of the Border clans and Lowland families have adopted the tartans first shown in the book.

## McIAN

Between 1845 and 1847 actor and illustrator Robert Ranald McIan published his drawings of Highland figures in a book called *The Clans of the Scottish Highlands.* The text was written by his friend and colleague James Logan (author of *The Scottish Gael,* 1831), who also supplied the patterns for the carefully detailed tartan costumes worn in the illustrations. McIan's prints became very popular in Victorian times and have remained so to this day. Some of the tartans depicted appear for the first time in McIan's work; others show minor variations now adopted by modern weavers.

*A McIan print of a figure in the Shaw Clan tartan, 1845.*

## W. & A. SMITH

William and Andrew Smith published the *Authenticated Tartans of the Clans and Families of Scotland* in 1850. They used setts from the pattern books of Meyer and Mortimer as well as from William Wilson & Sons, which were two of the leading weaving firms of the period.

## JAMES GRANT

James Grant was the author of *The Tartans and the Clans of Scotland,* which was published in 1886. The book contained the first illustration of the "Hunting Stewart". Grant based his illustrations on actual samples of tartans that were in use at the time of publication.

## D. W. STEWART

D. W. Stewart's *Old and Rare Scottish Tartans,* published in 1893 by George P. Johnston of Edinburgh, is now in itself a rare and valuable collectors' item. Stewart recorded just 45 tartans of particular interest or antiquity. Each tartan was specially woven in silk. Only 300 copies of the book were produced, of which 50 were in a special deluxe edition.

## W. AND A. K. JOHNSTON

The two-volume *The Tartans of the Clans and Septs of Scotland* contains over 200 tartans, including many hunting and dress setts illustrated for the first time. The book is a much expanded version of Henry Whyte's earlier work *The Scottish Clans and Their Tartans* which was published in 1891. The 1906 volumes include contributions from several authors, of which Henry Whyte was one. W. and A. K. Johnston continued to produce pocket books of tartans which were published annually for many years.

## DONALD C. STEWART

Following in the footsteps of his father, D. W. Stewart, whose *Old and Rare Scottish Tartans* had been published in 1893, Donald C. Stewart published *The Setts of the Scottish Tartans* in 1950. This was the first major attempt to record the threads and colours of all the tartans since Logan's work in 1831. By the second edition, published in 1974, the book contained 261 patterns under 134 names.

*The MacDonald Clan tartan.*

# TARTANS DIRECTORY

## *ABERCROMBIE FAMILY TARTAN*

**EARLIEST KNOWN DATE:**
1819
**EARLIEST RECORDED SOURCE:**
Logan, 1831
**STATUS:**
Recorded
**TYPE:**
Symmetrical

The earliest reference to a tartan named Abercrombie is in the pattern books of William Wilson & Sons of Bannockburn. It was a popular pattern, and Wilson produced it in various colours. "Aberc'by with yellow" and "Aberc'by with red" were sold alongside the Abercrombie with a white stripe, which we now know as Menteith district tartan. The version that Logan published as a clan tartan in 1831 could be described as Black Watch with white; it had also gained black tramlines in the blue ground colour. Weavers normally double Logan's thread count for the blue area to bring the proportions into line with the generally accepted form for kilt-making. The Abercrombie family takes its name from the lands of Abercrombie ("beyond the bend") of Fifeness. The head of the family is represented by the Abercrombies of Birkenbog.

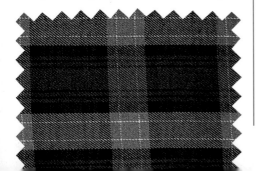

## *ANDERSON FAMILY TARTAN*

**EARLIEST KNOWN DATE:**
*c.* 1906
**EARLIEST RECORDED SOURCE:**
Johnston, 1906
**STATUS:**
Recorded
**TYPE:**
Symmetrical

This tartan can be traced back to *The Tartans of the Clans and Septs of Scotland,* published by W. and A. K. Johnston. It has since appeared in several similar forms, collected by James Cant and John MacGregor Hastie. These men were avid tartan collectors between 1930 and 1950 and provided much material for the cloth archive of the Scottish Tartans Society. They were inclined to collect aberrant varieties, and neither left very clear details of their sources. As a result there were 10 variations in the Scottish Tartans Society Collection. The sett illustrated is identical with the 1906 plate.

## ANGUS DISTRICT TARTAN

**EARLIEST KNOWN DATE:**
pre-1906
**EARLIEST RECORDED SOURCE:**
Johnston, 1906
**STATUS:**
Recorded
**TYPE:**
Symmetrical

It is not clear whether the Angus tartan was intended as a district or as a family tartan, and in consequence it has been used as both. It is now firmly established as a tartan for all those people having a connection with the area. The name Angus means "the one and only" possibly in reference to Angus, King of Dalriada in western Scotland in the 9th century. The name is associated with Clan MacInnes, who also claim descent from the Dalriada Scots. The earldom of Angus was held by the Stewarts and Douglases but is now vested in the dukedom of Hamilton.

## ARMSTRONG CLAN TARTAN

**EARLIEST KNOWN DATE:**
1842
**EARLIEST RECORDED SOURCE:**
*Vestiarium Scoticum*, 1842
**STATUS:**
Recorded
**TYPE:**
Symmetrical

The Armstrong tartan is a traditional design of green, black and blue with a single red stripe on the blue. An act passed by the Scottish parliament in 1587 refers to the Border clans, but the use of the term "clan" has a different meaning in the Lowland context, where the family structure was feudal in nature. Armstrongs claim descent from Fairbairn, armour bearer to an ancient king of Scotland, who granted him land in the Borders. The first gathering of Armstrongs for 400 years was held at Tourneyholm in Liddesdale in 1979.

## BAILLIE CLAN TARTAN

**EARLIEST KNOWN DATE:**
1800
**EARLIEST RECORDED SOURCE:**
Wilson's pattern book, 1819
**STATUS:**
Recorded
**TYPE:**
Symmetrical

Baillie is a military tartan similar to those of the MacLeods, the MacKenzies and the Campbells — all variations of the basic Black Watch regimental sett. The Baillie fencibles were disbanded in 1802, and it has been suggested that it was the white stripe of the MacKenzie, turned yellow with age, that became the Baillie tartan some years later — scoured but unbleached wool turns yellow after a few years. This is discounted by an entry in Wilson's manuscript notebooks of 1800, which states that "this was the sett in which the Baillie fencibles were clothed".

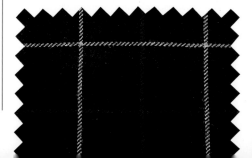

## BAIRD CLAN TARTAN

**EARLIEST KNOWN DATE:**
1906
**EARLIEST RECORDED SOURCE:**
Johnston, 1906
**STATUS:**
Recorded
**TYPE:**
Symmetrical

This tartan is first recorded in Johnston's work of 1906, and the sample from the Highland Society of London probably dates from the same period. In both these early references the triple stripes are rendered in red. Today, however, they are generally woven in purple. The name Baird originates from "bard", meaning poet.

## BISSET CLAN TARTAN

**EARLIEST KNOWN DATE:**
1976
**EARLIEST RECORDED SOURCE:**
Scottish Tartans Society, 1976
**STATUS:**
Registered with the Scottish Tartans Society, 1977
**TYPE:**
Symmetrical

One of the first tartans to be designed by the Scottish Tartans Society. Mrs Elizabeth Bisset gave the Society the following details for the colours of the sett: "The blue and white of the Bisset shield, yellow and black representing the motto, red for the 'eternal flame' and the local tartan; all on a green background." The motto of the Bissets is *Abscissa virescit*, meaning "Cut me down and I shall grow again". The yellow represents the wood chips from the axe and the green the fresh new growth. Bissets are represented in the histories of prominent Scottish families through the female line, with the result that the incidence of the Bisset surname has greatly diminished. There is no chief of the family at present (1993), but the senior branch are the Bissets of Lessendrum in Aberdeenshire.

## BARCLAY DRESS CLAN TARTAN

**EARLIEST KNOWN DATE:**
1906
**EARLIEST RECORDED SOURCE:**
Johnston, 1906
**STATUS:**
Recorded
**TYPE:**
Symmetrical

This tartan is based on the earlier hunting sett, which appeared in the *Vestiarium Scoticum* in 1842. Barclays appear to have no "regular" tartan, and the hunting version assumes this role and is the sett most commonly associated with the name. A yellow version of the same pattern appeared in Johnston's publication in 1906 and this is known as the dress Barclay tartan.

## BRODIE CLAN TARTAN

**EARLIEST KNOWN DATE:**
1850
**EARLIEST RECORDED SOURCE:**
Smith, 1850
**STATUS:**
Certified but undated; Highland Society of London Collection
**TYPE:**
Symmetrical

The origins of the Brodie tartan are difficult to pin down. The earliest and most reliable source is the original manuscript for the Smiths' book, *Authenticated Tartans of the Clans and Families of Scotland* (1850), although the sett was not included in the published work. The Smiths' sources included the findings of George Hunter, an army clothier, who toured the Highlands in search of old tartans before 1822. D. W. Stewart confirms this date but also mentions that the Brodies in Aberdeenshire wore the Huntly district tartan prior to 1820. There are also a different and more colourful sett, recorded in the *Baronage of Angus and Mearns* by David MacGregor Peter (1856), and a hunting sett, published in Whyte's *The Scottish Clans and Their Tartans* (1891).

## BRUCE CLAN TARTAN

**EARLIEST KNOWN DATE:**
1842
**EARLIEST RECORDED SOURCE:**
*Vestiarium Scoticum*, 1842
**STATUS:**
Approved by the clan chief, 1967
**TYPE:**
Symmetrical

The design comes from the *Vestiarium Scoticum* and is approved by Lord Bruce, Earl of Elgin. Much doubt has been cast on the authority of the *Vestiarium*, but Lord Bruce believes that he has independent evidence for this tartan dating from 1571. The original document was a chart of the weaver's thread count, which is now lost. The chart included black guards on the yellow and white stripes, and Lord Bruce has adopted this variation as his personal tartan. Writing in 1967, Lord Bruce stated that the Elgin family also wear the Bruce of Kinnaird for "undress" or day wear, which is a wholly different tartan, similar to the Prince Charles Edward.

# BUCHAN DISTRICT TARTAN

**EARLIEST KNOWN DATE:**
1790
**EARLIEST RECORDED SOURCE:**
Scottish Tartans Museum artifact, 1790
**STATUS:**
Approved by the chief, 1965
**TYPE:**
Asymmetrical

The tartan, which is also known as Cumming and as MacIntyre and Glenorchy, was adopted by the Buchan family around 1965, on account of their long association with the Cummings, an association that began with the marriage of Margaret, daughter of King Edgar, to William Coymen, sheriff of Forfar in 1210.

The name Buchan, although a family name, is territorial in origin. The sett is asymmetrical, although this is not immediately obvious. A single narrow blue stripe upsets the otherwise regular symmetrical pattern (see page 14). There is a sample in the Collection of the Highland Society of London, housed in the Scottish National Museum in Edinburgh.

# BUCHANAN CLAN TARTAN

**EARLIEST KNOWN DATE:**
1831
**EARLIEST RECORDED SOURCE:**
Mclan illustration, 1847
**STATUS:**
Recorded
**TYPE:**
Asymmetrical

There is some discussion in the archives of the Scottish Tartans Society about the suggestion that Mclan may be responsible for the change to an asymmetric sett from Logan's earlier symmetrical version. However, it appears that William Wilson, the foremost weaver of the time, may have agreed with Mclan and favoured the unusual asymmetrical design.

# The Tartans of Clan Cameron

The Cameron Clan tartans include some of the oldest and some of the most modern. According to Lt. Col. I. B. Cameron Taylor, the oldest authentic Clan Cameron tartan is the chief's own Cameron of Locheil. Its authenticity is vouched for by the remarkable posthumous portrait of the 19th chief, "Gentle" Locheil, painted by George Chalmers in 1764, which hangs at Achnacarry, the seat of the clan in Lochaber. The work was carried out some 16 years after the chief had died in exile in France and tartan had been banned in the Highlands as a result of the '45. The artist must have been aware of the historical significance of his work in the light of the deliberate attempts to suppress the spirit and identity of the warring Highlanders. The tartan, with its name and its clan association, is one of the very few that can be historically established around the time of the '45.

One of the most modern clan tartans is the Cameron Hunting. Preparing for the clan gathering at Achnacarry in 1956, Lt. Col. Cameron Taylor wrote: "The Hunting Cameron tartan follows what can now be regarded as the traditional evolution. It is based on the clan tartan (from the *Vestiarium Scoticum*) with the red changed to blue and with two green guard lines inserted round the yellow stripe." The choice of blue has a historical precedent. Cameron clansmen are described in a document in Latin 1689 as "the Lochaber men . . . clad in blue and yellow when they followed their great chief, Sir Ewan Cameron, to battle and victory at Killiecrankie". The new sett was first proposed by a J. G. MacKay of Portree, a noted antiquary and author of *The Romantic Story of the Highland Garb and Tartan*. Lt. Col. Cameron Taylor writes: "Although the origins, like so many of our tartans, are obscure, the present design is a happy one. It fulfils the need for a subdued Cameron tartan, whilst maintaining tradition and an interesting historical clan link with far off days."

One of the benefits of the new hunting sett has been to release the Cameron of Erracht from that role, so that it may be reserved solely as a regimental tartan for its rightful wearers, The Queen's Own Cameron Highlanders.

The regular Cameron clan tartan, which is readily available today, was first illustrated in the *Vestiarium Scoticum* in 1842.

The long history of the Clan Cameron tartans demonstrates the continuing tradition of tartan as part of the living and evolving fabric of Scotland.

## CAMERON CLAN TARTAN

**EARLIEST KNOWN DATE:**
1842 .
**EARLIEST RECORDED SOURCE:**
*Vestiarium Scoticum*, 1842
**STATUS:**
Approved by the chief, 1956
**TYPE:**
Symmetrical

The regular Clan Cameron tartan, which is readily available today, was first illustrated in the *Vestiarium Scoticum* in 1842, but did not come into wide use until the latter part of the Victorian era. It may be that the authors of this book were aware of earlier samples of the Cameron tartan, for the design they produced, claiming the authority of an ancient manuscript, has some similarity. These samples exist in the Cockburn Collection *c.* 1810–15 and the Collection of the Highland Society of London, *c.* 1816.

## CAMERON OF LOCHIEL TARTAN

**EARLIEST KNOWN DATE:**
1764
**EARLIEST RECORDED SOURCE:**
Smith, 1850
**STATUS:**
Approved by the chief, 1956
**TYPE:**
Symmetrical

This is the oldest of the Cameron Clan Tartans. In Smith's book, the design was illustrated with blue lines bordering the white, although these guard lines are now generally black. It is featured in a portrait of the 19th chief, painted posthumously in 1764 by George Chalmers, which is now at Achnacarry, the clan seat in Lochaber.

# The Tartans of Clan Campbell

The plain green, black and blue sett is worn by the MacCailein Mor, Chief of the Campbells, and his family, along with most of the principal Campbell families of Argyll. The same tartan, usually woven in darker shades, is also called the Government, 42nd, Military, Sutherland or Black Watch. The largest weaving company in Scotland during the 18th century, Wilson of Bannockburn, used the sett as a background and added different coloured stripes to distinguish the various clans and regiments. The Campbells of Argyll had yellow and white added and this was the preferred tartan of George, 6th Duke of Argyll (d. 1839). The 7th Duke, John (d. 1847), wore the tartan with white lines, now known as Lamont. The tartans of the Campbells of Breadalbane, Cawdor and Loudoun all have military origins. Other Campbell tartans exist, but only the ones illustrated here have the approval of the clan chief.

## CAMPBELL CLAN TARTAN

**EARLIEST KNOWN DATE:**
1725
**EARLIEST RECORDED SOURCE:**
Cockburn Collection, 1810–20
**STATUS:**
Approved by MacCailein Mor, Duke of Argyll
**TYPE:**
Symmetrical

The tartan appointed for the Highland Companies in 1725 and for the Black Watch in 1739 may have been worn by the Campbells at an earlier date. There is a strong probability that many others wore the sett or something similar before the idea of distinctive clan tartans took hold. General Wade (1673–1748), it is said, required a uniform that was different from the red coats of the regular soldier and that would be acceptable to the ranks formed from several Highland clans. Whatever the origins of this second most popular tartan (the Royal Stewart holds first place), it is now the official tartan of all the Campbells, approved by MacCailien Mor himself.

## CAMPBELL OF BREADALBANE CLAN TARTAN

**EARLIEST KNOWN DATE:**
c. 1810–20
**EARLIEST RECORDED SOURCE:**
Cockburn Collection, 1810–20
**STATUS:**
Approved by MacCailein Mor, Duke of Argyll
**TYPE:**
Symmetrical

The earliest sample of this pattern is called simply Breadalbane. W. and A. Smith (1850) were the first to illustrate the sett in its present form and they obtained the thread count from a specimen given by the Marquis of Breadalbane. D. W. Stewart illustrated a slightly different version, which he deduced from "a portion of the regimental uniform of Major Campbell, now treasured as a precious relic". Major Campbell was an officer of the district fencibles between 1793 and 1802.

## CAMPBELL OF CAWDOR CLAN TARTAN

**EARLIEST KNOWN DATE:**
1798
**EARLIEST RECORDED SOURCE:**
"Argyle" in Wilson letter, 1798
**STATUS:**
Approved by MacCailein Mor, Duke of Argyll
**TYPE:**
Symmetrical

Campbell of Cawdor is one of Wilson's variations based on the military sett. It was originally a numbered pattern, acquiring the name Argyle in 1798 and Argylle in 1819. It is not until W. and A. Smith's work of 1850 that the full title, Campbell of Cawdor, is given. There is a story that the Campbells became Lords of Cawdor by kidnapping the heiress of the Thane of Cawdor as a child and marrying her, 10 years later, to one of the Earl of Argyll's sons. This sett is authorized by the present clan chief of the Campbells, MacCailein Mor.

## CAMPBELL OF LOUDOUN CLAN TARTAN

**EARLIEST KNOWN DATE:**
1886
**EARLIEST RECORDED SOURCE:**
Grant, 1886
**STATUS:**
Approved by MacCailein Mor, Duke of Argyll
**TYPE:**
Symmetrical

The rarest of the Campbell tartans, Loudoun is, nevertheless, acknowledged by MacCailein Mor, chief of the Clan Campbell. It is similar to the Campbell of Argyll except for a different arrangement of black tramlines on the blue stripe. The tartan may have its origin in the formation of Loudoun's Highlanders, which were raised at the time of the '45 and disbanded in 1748, although a similar claim is made for another sett. The weavers, Wilson of Bannockburn, produced many variations of the Black Watch for the Highland regiments by adding coloured stripes to the basic pattern. The sett was not published until 1886, when James Grant included it in his book.

## CHATTAN CHIEF CLAN TARTAN

**EARLIEST KNOWN DATE:**
1816
**EARLIEST RECORDED SOURCE:**
Logan, 1831
**STATUS:**
Lyon Court Register, 1947
**TYPE:**
Symmetrical

This tartan is also known as Finzean's Fancy. The record of the Lord Lyon states: "Note – this tartan is specifically for the Chief of Clan Chattan and his immediate family." Logan described this sett (without the chief's extra white line) thus: "The Chief also wears a particular tartan of a very showy pattern." It was illustrated by W. and A. Smith in 1850. Chief of the Clan Chattan, Sir Aeneas Mackintosh of that Ilk, acknowledged this sett in 1816. Chattan is a clan confederation.

## CHISHOLM CLAN TARTAN

**EARLIEST KNOWN DATE:**
1842
**EARLIEST RECORDED SOURCE:**
*Vestiarium Scoticum,* 1842
**STATUS:**
Recorded
**TYPE:**
Symmetrical

The Chisholm clan tartan was also recorded by Frank Adam in *The Clans, Septs and Regiments of the Scottish Highlands,* published in 1908. Although the *Vestiarium Scoticum* has been discredited as an authentic source, many of the tartans it contains appear to be based on genuine older sets — in this case the Black Watch. There is a specimen of both Chisholm and Chisholm Hunting in the Collection of the Highland Society of London.

## CLARK FAMILY TARTAN

**EARLIEST KNOWN DATE:**
1847
**EARLIEST RECORDED SOURCE:**
Wilson's pattern book, 1847
**STATUS:**
Recorded
**TYPE:**
Symmetrical

This version of the Clark tartan is not widely known. The idea that Clarks dress in the sombre tones of the usual Clark tartan which follows is dispelled by this colourful design. A variation in Wilson's pattern books includes a further dark overcheck in the red square.

## CLERK, CLERGY, PRIEST

**EARLIEST KNOWN DATE:**
1831
**EARLIEST RECORDED SOURCE:**
Wilson's pattern book, 1847
**STATUS:**
Recorded
**TYPE:**
Symmetrical

This tartan is called, variously, Clark, Clerk, Clerke, Clergy and Priest within books dating from around 1850. Wilson called the tartan Priest in his 1847 pattern book. The muted colours conform to the Victorian idea of suitable clothing for the clergy. This is the tartan usually associated with the Clark family.

## COCHRANE CLAN TARTAN

**EARLIEST KNOWN DATE:**
1934
**EARLIEST RECORDED SOURCE:**
William Anderson, Edinburgh, 1934
**STATUS:**
Lyon Court Book (Appendix), 1984
**TYPE:**
Symmetrical

The earliest reference to this tartan is a sample woven by Messrs William Anderson of Edinburgh (now Kinloch Anderson) in 1934, which is now in the cloth archives of the Scottish Tartans Society. Lord Dundonald registered a version missing a red stripe with the Lord Lyon in 1974. There is a story that a fragment of this design, thought to be of greater authenticity, was discovered in the foundations of a Perthshire house around the 1930s. Other reports, however, suggest that the missing stripe was simply a typing error. The sett is based on the old Lochaber district tartan, which also provided a base for the MacDonald and the Cameron of Erracht, both of which have four red stripes. The red stripe has been restored in this version, which is now the approved tartan and appears in the Appendix of the Lyon Court Book, dated 12 November 1984.

## COCKBURN CLAN TARTAN

**EARLIEST KNOWN DATE:**
1819
**EARLIEST RECORDED SOURCE:**
Johnston, 1906
**STATUS:**
Recorded
**TYPE:**
Symmetrical

A curious mistake, which perhaps throws light on the use of names for tartans, was made in the identification of the Cockburn sett in the Cockburn Collection (c. 1810–20). Sir William Cockburn of Cockburn himself labelled a specimen of his own tartan, which was later discovered to be the MacKenzie, the tartan worn by the 71st Highland Light Infantry in which he served. The label has since been removed. It is fairly certain that a distinct Cockburn sett was in production at the time (1815), which was later recorded in Wilson's pattern books (1819). The sett in use today varies considerably from the old pattern in terms of proportion but retains the distinctive red, yellow and white stripes.

## COLQUHOUN CLAN TARTAN

**EARLIEST KNOWN DATE:**
c. 1810–20
**EARLIEST RECORDED SOURCE:**
Cockburn Collection, 1810–20
**STATUS:**
Certified by the chief, c. 1816
**TYPE:**
Symmetrical

The Banks and Braes of Loch Lomond were the setting for the interesting and sometimes violent history of the Colquhouns of Luss. Their tartan is well documented, appearing in the earliest collections, and it was certified by the chief, with his seal and signature, in the archives of the Highland Society of London in about 1816. In its present form the clan tartan was woven by Wilson of Bannockburn at the beginning of the 19th century and was recorded in the firm's 1819 pattern books. Wilson often used purple in place of blue and produced proportionately equivalent patterns in different weights of cloth. Logan recorded a similar sett in 1831. The *Vestiarium Scoticum* shows a pattern with the white stripe next to the blue, but this is regarded as an error.

## COMYN OR MACAULAY CLAN TARTAN

**EARLIEST KNOWN DATE:**
1845
**EARLIEST RECORDED SOURCE:**
Smith, 1850
**STATUS:**
Approved by the chief, 1850
**TYPE:**
Symmetrical

This sett resembles the earlier *Vestiarium Scoticum* version, which has an extra narrow red stripe on the green square, but is in fact the one given by Logan as MacAuley and illustrated by McIan in *The Clans of the Scottish Highlands* in 1845–7. W. and A. Smith wrote in the *Authenticated Tartans of the Clans and Families of Scotland* (1850) that the sett had the approval of the head of the family of Cumming. Comyns, Cummins and Cummings are all descendants of the Clan Comyn. Branches of the clan have changed the spelling and Cumming is now the most usual form of the name. Comyns once held the earldom of Buchan and the green Comyn tartan, which is quite different from the red, has been adopted by the Buchan family.

## CRAWFORD CLAN TARTAN

**EARLIEST KNOWN DATE:**
1842
**EARLIEST RECORDED SOURCE:**
*Vestiarium Scoticum,* 1842
**STATUS:**
Recorded
**TYPE:**
Symmetrical

From a 1739 story about the early days of the Black Watch we know that at that time there was no Crawford tartan. The first record of this sett is in the *Vestiarium Scoticum,* and it would appear that the tartan was designed between 1739 and 1842.

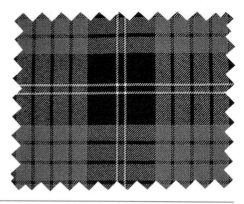

## DALZIEL FAMILY TARTAN

**EARLIEST KNOWN DATE:**
1831
**EARLIEST RECORDED SOURCE:**
Logan, 1831
**STATUS:**
Recorded
**TYPE:**
Symmetrical

The Dalziel or Dalzell tartan is similar to the Munro — too similar for coincidence, in fact. It is more probably the result of Wilson's *ad hoc* method of naming the genuine patterns he discovered in the course of business. The basic form of the design was used for a "George IV" tartan produced in honour of the king's visit to Scotland in 1822. The barony of Dalzell in Lanarkshire is the origin of the name. In Old Scots it means "I dare", and this is also the motto on the family coat of arms.

## DAVIDSON CLAN TARTAN

**EARLIEST KNOWN DATE:**
1822
**EARLIEST RECORDED SOURCE:**
D. W. Stewart, 1893
**STATUS:**
Certified by the chief, 1822
**TYPE:**
Symmetrical

D. C. Stewart called this sett "the more recent Davidson" and the basis for the Henderson tartan. It was published by his father, D. W. Stewart, in 1893 in *Old and Rare Scottish Tartans*. This version omits the white stripe of earlier setts recorded in the Collection of the Highland Society of London (1822) and in Moy Hall Collection. The Moy Hall Collection is kept by MacKintosh of MacKintosh at Moy Hall, near Inverness. Uniquely among tartans, there is a Half Davidson and a Double Davidson. The Half Davidson is a reduced pattern, while in the Double Davidson, a version woven by Wilson of Bannockburn around 1847, the red and white stripes are doubled.

## DOUGLAS CLAN TARTAN

**EARLIEST KNOWN DATE:**
pre-1831
**EARLIEST RECORDED SOURCE:**
Logan, 1831
**STATUS:**
Recorded
**TYPE:**
Symmetrical

Wilson sent a list of tartans to James Logan about 1830, stating that No. 148 had been sold as Douglas for a "considerable" time. There are many historic references to the Border clans, which would certainly describe the Douglases. There is also a black and grey sett for the clan, which first appeared in the *Vestiarum Scoticum*. The present chiefship is vacant because of the compound surnames of the eligible claimants: the Lord Lyon will not recognize double-barrelled names.

## DRUMMOND CLAN TARTAN

**EARLIEST KNOWN DATE:**
(1745), 1816
**EARLIEST RECORDED SOURCE:**
Logan, 1831
**STATUS:**
Certified by the chief
**TYPE:**
Symmetrical

Drummonds sometimes wore the tartan that is now known as Grant, and the Drummonds of Strathallen wore the Ogilvie as their tartan. This pattern is the Drummond of Perth, believed to have been worn by Bonnie Prince Charlie as a cloak during the '45. The overall appearance of the tartan links it to Perthshire, but closer inspection reveals elements of the Royal Stewart. A sample labelled "Perth (Grant/Drummond)" appears in the Certified Tartans volume in the Collection of the Highland Society of London dating from 1816.

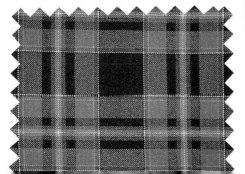

## DUNBAR FAMILY TARTAN

**EARLIEST KNOWN DATE:**
1842
**EARLIEST RECORDED SOURCE:**
*Vestiarium Scoticum*, 1842
**STATUS:**
Recorded
**TYPE:**
Symmetrical

The sett for this Lowland family first appeared in the *Vestiarium Scoticum,* and a Dunbar district tartan was woven by Wilson around 1850. It is not possible to say whether Wilson's pattern was intended as a district or a family sett. The current chief is Sir Jean Dunbar of Mochrum, who lives in Florida, USA.

## DUNDAS CLAN TARTAN

**EARLIEST KNOWN DATE:**
1842
**EARLIEST RECORDED SOURCE:**
*Vestiarium Scoticum,* 1842
**STATUS:**
Recorded
**TYPE:**
Symmetrical

The design has the traditional green, black and blue background of the Highland military tartans, with twin red stripes on the green. Members of the Dundas family played an important role in restoring the Highland way of life after the penalties imposed as a result of the '45. It was Henry Dundas, who, in 1784, introduced the Bill to Parliament to restore the estates forfeited to the Crown after the uprising, following the repeal of the Act of Proscription in 1782. The chief today is Sir David Dundas of Dundas.

## ELLIOT CLAN TARTAN

**EARLIEST KNOWN DATE:**
pre-1906
**EARLIEST RECORDED SOURCE:**
Johnston, 1906
**STATUS:**
Recorded
**TYPE:**
Symmetrical

The colouring of the Elliot tartan is unique among traditional tartans, being described as maroon and blue. The Elliots are a Border clan, founders of the Minto family. The chiefship once belonged to the Elliots of Redheugh but passed to the Elliots of Stobs near Hawick in Roxburghshire. The present chief is Mrs Margaret Elliot of that Ilk.

## ERSKINE CLAN TARTAN

**EARLIEST KNOWN DATE:**
1842
**EARLIEST RECORDED SOURCE:**
*Vestiarium Scoticum,* 1842
**STATUS:**
Recorded
**TYPE:**
Symmetrical

The Erskine clan or family originated in Renfrewshire. The first published version of the tartan appeared in the *Vestiarium Scoticum.* Cunningham tartan, which was published in the same work, differs from the Erskine sett only by the addition of a white stripe between the narrow green lines. The similarity of the design to the MacGregor tartan provides a tenuous connection which is, however, of little help in explaining the Erskine design.

## FARQUHARSON CLAN TARTAN

**EARLIEST KNOWN DATE:**
1774
**EARLIEST RECORDED SOURCE:**
Wilson's pattern book, 1819
**STATUS:**
Public Register of All Arms and Bearings, 1946
**TYPE:**
Symmetrical

The tartan was first published in James Logan's *Scottish Gael or Celtic Manners, as Preserved among the Highlanders* (1831). Four small pieces of this tartan were exhibited by Miss Farquharson of Invercauld at the Highland Exhibition held in Inverness in 1930. They were dated 1774. A specimen in the Highland Society of London Collection bears the seal of Farquharson of Finzean, *c.* 1816. The tartan can be distinguished from MacEwen, Rollo and MacLeod by the red and yellow stripes with black guard lines, and the red and yellow without guard lines running alternately across the fabric. Farquharsons were prominent Jacobites who fought in both the 1715 and 1745 uprisings. The present chief is Captain Alwynne Farquharson of Invercauld.

## FERGUSON CLAN TARTAN

**EARLIEST KNOWN DATE:**
1831
**EARLIEST RECORDED SOURCE:**
Logan, 1831
**STATUS:**
Approved by the clan chief, 1977
**TYPE:**
Symmetrical

The version of the Ferguson clan tartan published by Logan in 1831 gives the red stripes only two threads, a minor divergence from the sett that was approved by the Clan Society. There is a marked similarity to the authentic, old Lochaber district tartan, which may have provided a basis for many of the clan tartans in that area. D. C. Stewart calls this the Ferguson of Balquhidder to distinguish it from the Ferguson of Atholl, which has a white stripe. The MacLarens, who were also followers of the Murrays of Atholl, have the Ferguson of Atholl design with a yellow stripe. Chiefs of the clan are the Fergussons of Kilkerran, the descendants of Fergus of Dalriada, who brought the Stone of Scone to Scotland. The present chief of the whole name is Sir Charles Fergusson of Kilkerran.

## FLETCHER FAMILY TARTAN

**EARLIEST KNOWN DATE:**
1906
**EARLIEST RECORDED SOURCE:**
Johnston, 1906
**STATUS:**
Recorded
**TYPE:**
Symmetrical

The tartan is sometimes called Fletcher of Saltoun, but it is commonly worn by all Scottish Fletchers, regardless of family origins. According to legend, *"Is e Clan-an-leisdeir a thog a cued amuid thug goil air uisge 'an Urcha".* ("It was the Fletcher Clan that first raised smoke and boiled their water in Glen Orchy.") The tartan is similar in design to the Old Lochaber district tartan, an area that includes Glen Orchy.

## FORBES CLAN TARTAN

**EARLIEST KNOWN DATE:**
*c.*1810–20
**EARLIEST RECORDED SOURCE:**
Wilson's pattern book, 1819
**STATUS:**
Recorded
**TYPE:**
Symmetrical

This is the Forbes sett in use today. It was said to have been designed by a Miss Forbes in 1822 for the Forbes family of Pitsligo, but earlier records would appear to discount this story. It appears in Wilson's 1819 pattern book. Smith (1850) and Grant (1886) also record this pattern. A different sett has been approved by the clan chief and registered with the Lord Lyon, possibly because of the similarity of this sett to the Lamont tartan. The registered pattern is known as Forbes Ancient.

## FRASER CLAN TARTAN

**EARLIEST KNOWN DATE:**
1816
**EARLIEST RECORDED SOURCE:**
*Vestiarium Scoticum,* 1842
**STATUS:**
Recorded
**TYPE:**
Symmetrical

Early references to this tartan include one by Wilson of Bannockburn, but Wilson did not name the sett. D. W. Stewart contended that it is, in fact, an early Grant tartan, which he traced to a portrait of Robert Grant of Lurg (1678–1771). It is undoubtedly the most popular Fraser pattern today. There is a Fraser Regimental tartan in the Collection of the Highland Society of London (volume 1), and a Fraser of Lovat in the Certified Tartans.

### GALBRAITH CLAN TARTAN

**EARLIEST KNOWN DATE:**
1816
**EARLIEST RECORDED SOURCE:**
Highland Society of London, 1816
**STATUS:**
Recorded
**TYPE:**
Symmetrical

It seems certain that the tartan was first known as Galbraith, although it is also named Russell, Hunter and Mitchell. John Telfer Dunbar, a noted expert on Highland dress, states that he has a record of a Hunter tartan designed by a gentleman named Hunter in 1824 but without a thread count. Wilson recorded it as Russell in 1847. The name Galbraith ("Briton's son" in Gaelic) is connected with the earls of Lennox, and at one time Galbraiths took protection from Clan Donald.

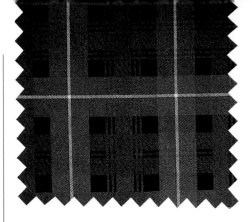

### GORDON REGIMENTAL TARTAN

**EARLIEST KNOWN DATE:**
1793
**EARLIEST RECORDED SOURCE:**
Wilson's pattern book, 1819
**STATUS:**
Approved by the chief
**TYPE:**
Symmetrical

Wilson of Bannockburn advertised a range of different quality Gordon tartans in the same colours. Forsythe of Huntly, acting as Wilson's agent, produced samples with one, two and three yellow stripes for the Duke of Gordon (some say for the Duchess), when he required new uniforms for the Gordon Highlanders in 1793. The Duke chose the single stripe and, according to Captain Wolrige-Gordon of Esslemont in recent research, the Gordon-Cummings took the two-stripe version and Esslemont the three stripes.

### GORDON OF ABERGELDIE FAMILY TARTAN

**EARLIEST KNOWN DATE:**
1723
**EARLIEST RECORDED SOURCE:**
Portrait at Abergeldie Castle, 1723
**STATUS:**
Lyon Court Book, 1953
**TYPE:**
Symmetrical

This sett was reconstructed from a scarf in a painting of Rachael Gordon, hanging in Abergeldie Castle, painted by Alexander in 1723. The count and colour description were taken by the Lord Lyon in 1953. It is often called the Red Gordon.

### GOW CLAN TARTAN

**EARLIEST KNOWN DATE:**
*c.*1815
**EARLIEST RECORDED SOURCE:**
Highland Society of London, *c.* 1815
**STATUS:**
Recorded
**TYPE:**
Symmetrical

This tartan can be seen in a portrait of Neil Gow by Sir Henry Raeburn (1756–1823). The design is like a simple form of the Robertson, and it may be the basis for the design of later tartans. The Gows or MacGowans were associated with the MacDonalds and the Clan Chattan. Gow is Gaelic for Smith, and the Hunting Gow is often worn by people of that name.

### GRAHAM OF MENTEITH CLAN TARTAN

**EARLIEST KNOWN DATE:**
1816
**EARLIEST RECORDED SOURCE:**
Logan, 1831
**STATUS:**
Recorded
**TYPE:**
Symmetrical

A piece of tartan described as Graham of Menteith "in a very small sett" appears in volume II of the Collection of the Highland Society of London. It came from the original box of certified tartans, but was among those "of which the seals were not legible . . . and damaged by moths". Logan (1831) describes the broad blue stripe as "smalt" in his book, and Smibert records this sett in 1850. The Menteith district tartan is similar, but the azure stripe is white.

### GRAHAM OF MONTROSE CLAN TARTAN

**EARLIEST KNOWN DATE:**
*c.*1810–20
**EARLIEST RECORDED SOURCE:**
Cockburn Collection, 1810–20
**STATUS:**
Certified by the chief, 1816
**TYPE:**
Symmetrical

D. C. Stewart has pointed out the similarity of this sett to the MacCallum tartan. The sample in the Collection of the Highland Society of London retains the signature and seal of the clan chief, dating from around 1816. This tartan is worn unofficially by 205 (Scottish Command) General Hospital Royal Army Medical Corps Volunteers.

## GRANT CLAN TARTAN

**EARLIEST KNOWN DATE:**
1831
**EARLIEST RECORDED SOURCE:**
Logan, 1831
**STATUS:**
Recorded
**TYPE:**
Symmetrical

The usual design is sometimes called Drummond. It was recorded by Logan (1831), Smibert (1850) and Smith (1850). Mclan's drawing of the Grant tartan is too roughly done to make out the pattern details. The difficulty of establishing a single Grant tartan to represent the clan is illustrated by the existence of 10 Grant portraits at Cullen House, Cullen, on the northeast coast of Scotland, in which each brother is wearing a different tartan, and, where a coat or plaid is worn, these also differ. In 1993, a modified version of the sett recorded by Logan was accredited by the Scottish Tartans Society for the Grants of Ballindalloch.

## GUNN CLAN TARTAN

**EARLIEST KNOWN DATE:**
c.1810–20
**EARLIEST RECORDED SOURCE:**
Cockburn Collection, 1810–20
**STATUS:**
Recorded
**TYPE:**
Symmetrical

The Cockburn Collection contains some of the oldest actual specimens of clan tartans in existence today. James Logan recorded the sett in his book in 1831, and it was one of the very few patterns not available to him from either the Highland Society or the samples sent by Wilson. The central blue stripes are often reproduced in black or very dark blue, giving the impression of four equally toned stripes. The Gunns come from the very north of Scotland.

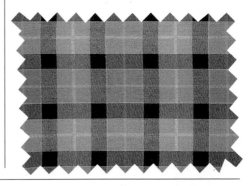

## HAMILTON (RED) CLAN TARTAN

**EARLIEST KNOWN DATE:**
1842
**EARLIEST RECORDED SOURCE:**
*Vestiarium Scoticum*, 1842
**STATUS:**
Recorded
**TYPE:**
Symmetrical

First recorded in the *Vestiarium Scoticum,* the original illustration shows the four main stripes in a very dark shade of blue. There is no evidence of a Hamilton tartan prior to the publication of this work. It is probable that the design can be attributed to Allan Hay (alias Charles Edward Stuart), who prepared the illustrations for the book.

## HANNAY FAMILY TARTAN

**EARLIEST KNOWN DATE:**
c.1810–44
**EARLIEST RECORDED SOURCE:**
Artifact, c. 1810–44
**STATUS:**
Lynn Court Book, 1984
**TYPE:**
Symmetrical

The Hannay tartan has been long established in the southwest of Scotland. An old kilt worn by Commander Alex Hannay (1788–1844) was discovered in a family chest by his descendant, Miss Anne Hannay, and came into the possession of Councillor John Hannay, a well-known tartan designer and collector. He created a new design based on the old. This sett was produced around 1950 by the weavers Galt of Galloway. The black and white check, a common feature of Lowland tartans, was originally woven with undyed wool and is found in the earliest of tartans, the Shepherd's Plaid.

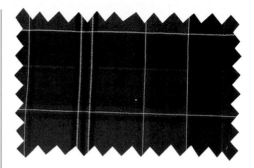

## HAY AND LEITH CLAN TARTAN

**EARLIEST KNOWN DATE:**
c.1810–20
**EARLIEST RECORDED SOURCE:**
Cockburn Collection, 1810–20
**STATUS:**
Recorded
**TYPE:**
Symmetrical

This distinctive and unusual pattern stands out from the pages of the Cockburn Collection as a design of particular colour and beauty. It most probably came from the looms of Wilson of Bannockburn, for the thread count is recorded later in the firm's 1819 pattern books. The Hay–Leith connection is believed to have come about through a marriage between the two families. At Delgaty Castle, Grampian, there is a Clan Hay centre. Leith Hall near Huntly, home of the Leith-Hays, is owned by the National Trust for Scotland.

## HENDERSON CLAN TARTAN

**EARLIEST KNOWN DATE:**
1906
**EARLIEST RECORDED SOURCE:**
Johnston, 1906
**STATUS:**
Recorded
**TYPE:**
Symmetrical

The name Henderson in Gaelic is MacEanruig, which is sometimes rendered as MacKendrick. Hendersons from the north are associated with the Clan Gunn and wear the Gunn tartan. Hendersons and MacKendricks from Lochaber and Angus wear their own sett, which in some ways resembles the Davidson. Both of these tartans were recorded by W. and A. K. Johnston.

## INNES (OF MORAY) CLAN TARTAN

**EARLIEST KNOWN DATE:**
1938
**EARLIEST RECORDED SOURCE:**
Innes, 1938
**STATUS:**
Lyon Court Register
**TYPE:**
Symmetrical

D. C. Stewart wrote: "Within recent years this sett has been accepted as the tartan appropriate to the Inneses of the Moray district." Sir Thomas Innes of Learney, the Lord Lyon, King of Arms, 1945–69, included this sett in his book the *Tartans of the Clans and Families of Scotland*, published in 1938 prior to his royal appointment. His younger son, Malcolm Innes of Edingight, became the Lord Lyon in 1981.

## JOHNSTON CLAN TARTAN

**EARLIEST KNOWN DATE:**
1842
**EARLIEST RECORDED SOURCE:**
*Vestiarium Scoticum*, 1842
**STATUS:**
Recorded
**TYPE:**
Symmetrical

The Johnstons were a powerful Border clan, who pursued a deadly feud with the Maxwells. Their stronghold was Lochwood Tower, near Beattock, which was burned down by the Maxwells in 1593. Before the publication of the *Vestiarium Scoticum* in 1842 Border tartans were generally unnamed. It is more likely the tartan came from the Aberdeenshire Johnstons, whose family seat is at Caskieben, Blackburn.

## KEITH AND AUSTIN CLAN TARTAN

**EARLIEST KNOWN DATE:**
1819
**EARLIEST RECORDED SOURCE:**
D. W. Stewart, 1893
**STATUS:**
Recorded
**TYPE:**
Symmetrical

This sett is based on the pattern recorded by Wilson of Bannockburn in 1819 as "No. 75 or Austin". D. W. Stewart recorded the version reproduced here in his book, *Old and Rare Scottish Tartans,* in which he wrote "it is included in every complete early collection". It does not, however, appear in the Cockburn Collection nor in the 1827 list of the Collection of the Highland Society. The earliest attribution is, therefore, given to Wilson. The Keiths

were a powerful Celtic family, who held the hereditary office of great marischal of Scotland. They are associated with Dunottar Castle, near Stonehaven.

## KENNEDY CLAN TARTAN

**EARLIEST KNOWN DATE:**
1845
**EARLIEST RECORDED SOURCE:**
Mclan illustratration, 1845
**STATUS:**
Recorded
**TYPE:**
Symmetrical

D. W. Stewart wrote, in 1893, that the design had been accepted by the Kennedy's of Carrick in the 18th century as an emblem of their Jacobite sympathies. The wearing of tartan in the Scottish Lowlands at this period in history would have been a very provocative gesture. The powerful Kennedy family were the earls of Cassilis, and they built the castles of Culzean and Dunure on the Ayrshire coast. A branch of the Kennedy family left the Ayrshire stronghold to settle in Lochaber where they were accepted as a sept by Clan Cameron. There is no similarity with the Cameron tartans.

## KERR CLAN TARTAN

**EARLIEST KNOWN DATE:**
1842
**EARLIEST RECORDED SOURCE:**
*Vestiarium Scoticum,* 1842
**STATUS:**
Recorded
**TYPE:**
Symmetrical

The Kerrs are believed to be of Viking descent, arriving in the Borders of Scotland by way of France and settling at Ferniehurst near Jedburgh, Borders. The heads of the family hold the title of marquesses of Lothian and now live at Monteviot. The true origin of the tartan is unknown, as the claims of antiquity in the *Vestiarium Scoticum* are doubtful.

## LAMONT CLAN TARTAN

**EARLIEST KNOWN DATE:**
*c.*1810–20
**EARLIEST RECORDED SOURCE:**
Cockburn Collection, 1810–20
**STATUS:**
Certified by the clan chief, 1817
**TYPE:**
Symmetrical

The Clan Lamont is closely associated with Clan Campbell, and the tartan now worn by the Lamonts is like the Campbell of Argyll, except that all the stripes on the green ground colour are white. A sample in the Collection of the Highland Society of London bears the seal and signature of the clan chief Lamont of Lamont, 9 January 1817. The sett is documented by Logan (1831), Smith (1850) and Grant (1886). The Lamont and Forbes tartans are identical except that in the Forbes there are black guards to the white line.

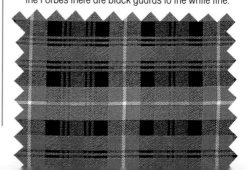

## LENNOX DISTRICT TARTAN

**EARLIEST KNOWN DATE:**
pre-1600
**EARLIEST RECORDED SOURCE:**
D. W. Stewart, 1893
**STATUS:**
Recorded
**TYPE:**
Symmetrical

Families with the surname Lennox are usually considered to be related to the Stewarts or the MacFarlanes and they wear the tartans of these clans. Other Lennox families prefer to wear the distinctive and ancient Lennox tartan, which is regarded as having a district origin. D. W. Stewart reproduced the sett from copies of the "lost" portrait of the Countess of Lennox dating from the 16th century. The Lennox, like the Old Lochaber and the numerous Hebridean district setts, is thought to have been the basis for many of the clan tartans that later became established.

## LESLIE HUNTING CLAN TARTAN

**EARLIEST KNOWN DATE:**
c. 1810–20
**EARLIEST RECORDED SOURCE:**
Cockburn Collection, 1810–20
**STATUS:**
Recorded
**TYPE:**
Symmetrical

This tartan is said to have been worn by George, 14th Earl of Rothes, who died in 1841. It is shown by Smibert (1850) and by W. and A. Smith (1850) but without the description "hunting". It has much in common with the Colquhoun tartan but for the position of the red stripe. There is also an unusual dress Leslie, which is predominantly red and which first appeared in the *Vestiarium Scoticum* (1842). The present chief of the clan is the Earl of Rothes.

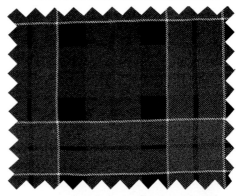

## LINDSAY CLAN TARTAN

**EARLIEST KNOWN DATE:**
1842
**EARLIEST RECORDED SOURCE:**
*Vestiarium Scoticum*, 1842
**STATUS:**
Recorded
**TYPE:**
Symmetrical

The Lindsay tartan is often first recognized by its colour, which is unusual because the precise shade of tartan colours is normally left to the discretion of the weaver. The sett is similar to Stewart of Atholl, but for the black, rendered in Lindsay as dark blue. The name Lindsay first appeared in the Borders in the 12th century.

## LIVINGSTONE CLAN TARTAN

**EARLIEST KNOWN DATE:**
Unknown
**EARLIEST RECORDED SOURCE:**
Bain, 1976
**STATUS:**
Recorded
**TYPE:**
Symmetrical

Robert Bain's *The Clans and Tartans of Scotland*, 1990, illustrates this sett, which is similar to the Stewart of Appin tartan. The small Highland clan of Livingstone, which comes from the Isle of Lismore and western Argyll, originally bore a Gaelic name spelled in different ways — MacDunsleinhe, *Mac-an-Leigh* (son of the physician) or Maclea — and was connected to the Stewarts of Appin. An alternative Livingstone or MacLay tartan is a variation of the MacLaine of Lochbuie sett. David Livingstone, the African missionary, was a descendant of the Livingstones of Argyll.

## LOGAN OR MACLENNAN CLAN TARTAN

**EARLIEST KNOWN DATE:**
1831
**EARLIEST RECORDED SOURCE:**
Logan, 1831
**STATUS:**
Recorded
**TYPE:**
Symmetrical

There is no authoritative explanation for the Logan–MacLennon connection. In his book *The Clans of Scotland*, published in 1991, Micheil MacDonald suggests that Logan (possibly Lobban) was an alternative name for MacLennan rather than a separate clan who shared a tartan. Alternative names or aliases are not uncommon in early Scottish records. Logans have another tartan, known also as Skene or Rose. Wilson produced a popular range of Logan tartans in the first half of the 19th century: Dark Logan had black in place of blue; Light Logan had pink stripes; and Logan with Yellow had yellow in place of the narrow purple stripes. It would seem that Wilson regarded Logan as a pattern type rather than as a distinctive sett.

# MacAlister Clan Tartan

**EARLIEST KNOWN DATE:**
1816
**EARLIEST RECORDED SOURCE:**
Smith, 1850
**STATUS:**
Certified by the chief, c. 1816
**TYPE:**
Symmetrical

This sett is taken from the manuscript of W. and A. Smith's *Authenticated Tartans of the Clans and Families of Scotland.* The Smiths' sources included the findings of George Hunter, an army clothier, who toured the Highlands in search of old tartans prior to 1822. MacAlisters are descendents of Donald of Islay, Lord of the Isles. Contemporary accounts of Flora MacDonald (1722–90) suggest that MacAlisters wore the MacDonald tartan at that time. The MacAlister tartan certified by the chief in 1816 is related to the MacDonald of Staffa in its design. Chief MacAlister of Loup was recognized by the Lord Lyon in 1991.

# MacAlister of Glenbarr Clan Tartan

**EARLIEST KNOWN DATE:**
c.1930
**EARLIEST RECORDED SOURCE:**
MacGregor Hastie Collection, 1930–50
**STATUS:**
Approved by Glenbarr, 1993
**TYPE:**
Symmetrical

This sample comes from the MacGregor Hastie Collection, which forms the basis of the cloth archive of the Scottish Tartans Society kept at Fonab House in Pitlochry. It is identical to the MacGillivray hunting tartan. This sett has been adopted by MacAlister Societies in the United States and Australia. The design is related to the MacDonald group of tartans, corresponding to the early lineage of the MacAlisters. The tartan is available from the Clan MacAlister Centre at Glenbarr, and is sold in aid of the restoration fund for the family seat.

## MacAlpine Clan Tartan

**EARLIEST KNOWN DATE:**
1908
**EARLIEST RECORDED SOURCE:**
Adam, 1908
**STATUS:**
Recorded
**TYPE:**
Asymmetrical

*The Clans, Sept and Regiments of the Scottish Highlands* (1908) by Frank Adam contains the first published record of the MacAlpine tartan. The history of the Clan MacAlpine is obscure. The Siol Alpin is claimed as the origin of a number of clans, but, as D. C. Stewart remarked, "[it] belongs rather to mythology than to history". It is considered to be a branch of the royal Clan Alpin, Kings of Dalriada. The tartan is similar to the hunting MacLean, but for the yellow line.

## MacArthur Clan Tartan

**EARLIEST KNOWN DATE:**
1842
**EARLIEST RECORDED SOURCE:**
*Vestiarium Scoticum,* 1842
**STATUS:**
Recorded
**TYPE:**
Symmetrical

At one time MacArthurs were linked with the MacDonalds, and this tartan has the same basic form as the MacDonald, Lord of the Isles sett. MacArthurs held land in Skye as the hereditary pipers to the MacDonalds. There is also an older MacArthur of Milton tartan, the design of which reflects the links with Clan Campbell.

## MacAulay Clan Tartan

**EARLIEST KNOWN DATE:**
1881
**EARLIEST RECORDED SOURCE:**
Logan/M'Intyre North, 1881
**STATUS:**
Recorded
**TYPE:**
Symmetrical

This shorter version tallies with the count published by M'Intyre North in 1881 as having been given to him by Logan. Smith (1850) calls it Comyn. There are two clans of the name associated with districts, although there is no family connection between them. They are the MacAuleys of Ardencaple, who are associated with the MacGregors, and the MacAulays of Lewis, who are associated with the MacLeods. In its shortened form this sett is closer to the MacGregor tartan.

## *MACBEAN CLAN TARTAN*

**EARLIEST KNOWN DATE:**
c.1815
**EARLIEST RECORDED SOURCE:**
McIan, 1845–7
**STATUS:**
Recorded
**TYPE:**
Symmetrical

MacBain, MacBean and MacVean are all forms of the same name, possibly from the same origin as the 11th-century Scottish king, Donald Ban. The principal family is MacBean of Kinchyle, from the northern end of Loch Ness. The MacBains are associated with the Mackintoshes, and this is apparent in the design of the tartan. This version, recorded by the Lord Lyon under the name MacBain, shows a variation on the earlier MacBean sett attributed to McIan.

## *MACBRIDE FAMILY TARTAN*

**EARLIEST KNOWN DATE:**
1992
**EARLIEST RECORDED SOURCE:**
Design: Harry Lindley, 1992
**STATUS:**
Accreditation pending
**TYPE:**
Symmetrical

The family of MacBride (from Saint Bride or Brigid) is known to have been a sept of the MacDonalds. Head of the family, Capt. Stuart C. MacBride, a member of the Weaver Incorporation of Aberdeen, commissioned Harry Lindley to create a MacBride tartan from the ensigns armorial recently granted by the Lord Lyon. Traditionally, members of the family, as a courtesy, ask permission of the chief or head of the family before wearing his tartan.

## *MACCOLL CLAN TARTAN*

**EARLIEST KNOWN DATE:**
1797
**EARLIEST RECORDED SOURCE:**
Wilson's pattern book, 1819
**STATUS:**
Recorded
**TYPE:**
Symmetrical

The MacColl tartan was produced by Wilson of Bannockburn in 1797 under the name Bruce, later known as Old Bruce. Some historical detective work was required to establish the earliest date for the MacColl tartan. The MacColls, a branch of the Clan Donald, settled around Loch Fyne. Some of the clan living in the Ballachulish area took protection from the Stewart of Appin. There is considerable similarity in the pattern structure of the Appin and the MacColl

designs. Wilson took great care to produce genuine Highland tartans but was less concerned with the naming of them, which suggests that he had, in fact, produced a MacColl tartan with a mistaken identity.

# The Tartans of Clan Donald

**Of the nine independent branches of the Clan Donald, there are at least 27
different setts. Clanranald, Glengarry, Sleat, and the earls of Antrim still
have chiefs, but for the MacDonalds known as the MacIains of
Ardnamurchan, the MacDonalds of Glencoe, the MacDonalds of Dunnyveg
and the Glens and the MacDonalds of Keppoch, the chiefship has become
vacant. Any other names associated with MacDonald tartans – like Staffa,
Boisdale or Kingsburgh are in fact cadets of the main branches. Staffa and
Boisdale are part of Clanranald and Kingsburgh is part of Sleat.
The Clan Donald empire in the Western Isles was divided in 1545 after the
death of Donald Dubh MacDonald, and it was not until 1947 that the
MacDonalds again had a high chief, MacDhomnuill, who by tradition has the
final word on the tartans of the clan. That right was granted to Alexander
MacDonald of MacDonald (formerly of Sleat), whose son Godfrey is now the
8th Chief of all the MacDonalds.**

## MACDONALD CLAN TARTAN

**EARLIEST KNOWN DATE:**
c. 1810–20
**EARLIEST RECORDED SOURCE:**
Cockburn Collection, 1810–20
**STATUS:**
Recorded
**TYPE:**
Symmetrical

This is the oldest recorded version of the clan sett.
Curiously, in the year that General Cockburn was
cataloguing his collection, 1815, Lord Macdonald
himself was, in his own words, "really ignorant of
what is exactly The MacDonald Tartan". In order to
reply to the Highland Society of London, he suggested
that Sir John Murray might be able to supply a
"perfectly genuine Pattern Such as Will Warrant me in
Authenticating it". The green, black and blue
background and the red stripe are based on the Old
Lochaber district sett.

## MACDONALD OF CLANRANALD CLAN TARTAN

**EARLIEST KNOWN DATE:**
1816
**EARLIEST RECORDED SOURCE:**
Smith, 1850
**STATUS:**
Public Register of All Arms, 1946
**TYPE:**
Symmetrical

This is the count from the Lord Lyon's records multiplied by four. It corresponds to the sett given by W. and A. Smith (1850) and in the work of J. Grant (1886). The tartan is distinguished by the two white lines. There is a certified example in the Collection of the Highland Society of London, c. 1816.

## MACDONALD OF STAFFA CLAN TARTAN

**EARLIEST KNOWN DATE:**
1816
**EARLIEST RECORDED SOURCE:**
Wilson's pattern book, 1819
**STATUS:**
Recorded
**TYPE:**
Symmetrical

Until recently the various branches of the Clan Donald were regarded as independent clans in their own right. The MacDonalds of Staffa are a cadet branch of Clanranald, but the Staffa tartan has more in common with the MacDonald of Sleat and the old Hebridean district setts.

## MACDONALD OF SLEAT CLAN TARTAN

**EARLIEST KNOWN DATE:**
c. 1815
**EARLIEST RECORDED SOURCE:**
Adam, 1908
**STATUS:**
Recorded
**TYPE:**
Symmetrical

The MacDonald of Sleat tartan was manufactured in the 18th century and called MacDonald of Sleat, Lord of the Isles. The pattern was devised from an old MacDonald tartan that is shown in a painting dating from before 1815 at Armadale Castle, probably at the instigation of Lord Macdonald, about 1815, but it appears that the reconstruction differs somewhat from the original. Whether this was intended or simply a mistake is entirely open to conjecture, but it would not be the first new design to have arisen from an error in the thread count.

## MACDONELL OF GLENGARRY CLAN TARTAN

**EARLIEST KNOWN DATE:**
c. 1816
**EARLIEST RECORDED SOURCE:**
Johnston, 1906
**STATUS:**
Certified by the chief, c. 1816
**TYPE:**
Symmetrical

The MacDonell of Glengarry tartan is the basic MacDonald sett with an additional white stripe. There is a sample certified by Glengarry in the Collection of the Highland Society of London from 1815–16, but it is not known if the thread count corresponds to the sett illustrated here. The Glengarry MacDonalds once held the ruined Castle at Invergarry in Lochaber.

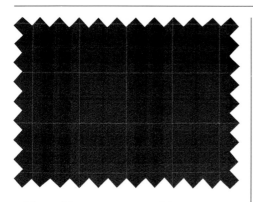

## MACDONELL OF KEPPOCH CLAN TARTAN

**EARLIEST KNOWN DATE:**
1893
**EARLIEST RECORDED SOURCE:**
D. W. Stewart, 1893
**STATUS:**
Recorded
**TYPE:**
Symmetrical

*Old and Rare Scottish Tartans* (1893) contains 45 setts that D. W. Stewart regarded as "being of special interest or antiquity". The Keppoch sett departs from the MacDonald and has more in common with the MacKintosh or the Robertson. These similarities support the idea that early tartan design owed more to territorial origin than to clan affiliation.

## MACDOUGALL CLAN TARTAN

**EARLIEST KNOWN DATE:**
1815–16
**EARLIEST RECORDED SOURCE:**
Paton's Collection, 1830
**STATUS:**
Certified by the chief, c. 1815
**TYPE:**
Symmetrical

The earliest reference to the MacDougall tartan is in the Collection of the Highland Society of London, where a sample exists, signed and sealed by the clan chief around 1815. The sett is a complex one, and the nearest count to the present tartan comes from a sample in Paton's Collection, which is housed at the Scottish Tartans Museum and dates from about 1830. The Highland Society also has a sample, certified by the Chief MacDougall of MacDougall and dated 1906, in its archives store at the Royal Caledonian School near London.

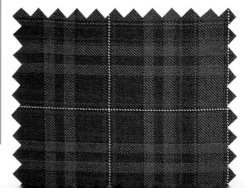

## MacDuff Clan Tartan

**EARLIEST KNOWN DATE:**
1816
**EARLIEST RECORDED SOURCE:**
Logan, 1831
**STATUS:**
Certified by the chief, c.1816
**TYPE:**
Symmetrical

According to D. C. Stewart, "it will be observed that the MacDuff tartan is substantially the Royal Stuart [sic] with the white and yellow lines removed. Whether this indicates it as a source of the Stuart [sic], or the association of the Earls of Fife with the Crown, remains to be determined". James Logan published this sett in his book in 1831.

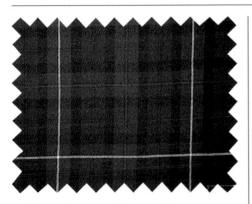

## MacEwan Clan Tartan

**EARLIEST KNOWN DATE:**
1906
**EARLIEST RECORDED SOURCE:**
Johnston, 1906
**STATUS:**
Recorded
**TYPE:**
Symmetrical

The tartan resembles the Campbell of Loudoun except for the red stripe. MacEwans have a historical association with the Campbells dating from 1432, when the lands of MacEwan of the Otter were annexed to Campbell territory. The association was not always a happy one, and the "broken" MacEwans settled in various parts of Lennox, Lochaber and Galloway. Elspeth MacEwan was the last witch to be burned at the stake, at Kirkcudbright in 1698.

## MacFarlane Clan Tartan

**EARLIEST KNOWN DATE:**
1816
**EARLIEST RECORDED SOURCE:**
Sash in Scottish Tartans Museum, 1822
**STATUS:**
Public Register of All Arms and Bearings, 1957
**TYPE:**
Symmetrical

The colours and threads of this pattern were taken from a silk, satin-weave sash, dated 1822, in the Collection of the Scottish Tartans Museum in Comrie, Perthshire. The sett varies slightly from the one registered with the Lord Lyon, but it is often the manufacturer's choice. Wilson produced this sett with purple in place of blue. Logan recorded the sett in 1831, as did Smibert (1850) and W. and A. Smith (1850). MacFarlanes, "sons of Parlan", were proscribed and their lands forfeited, in the same way as the MacGregors. Many emigrated and some changed their name – Bartholomew is a form of the name. At present there is no chief of the MacFarlanes.

## MacGillivray Clan Tartan

**EARLIEST KNOWN DATE:**
1816
**EARLIEST RECORDED SOURCE:**
Logan, 1831
**STATUS:**
Certified by the chief, c.1816
**TYPE:**
Symmetrical

"A characteristic Clan Chattan tartan," wrote D. C. Stewart, "with much in common with the setts of the neighbouring clans in Strathnairn and Morvern." Wilson produced this sett with a black stripe in the centre of the red square. The hunting MacGillivray is identical to the MacAlister of Glenbarr (see page 47). Gilli stems from *gille* in Gaelic, meaning "servant", in this case *gille bhrath*, "servant of judgement". MacGillivrays pledged allegiance to the MacKintosh

chiefs and fought on the side of the Jacobites in 1715 and 1745. The chiefship is vacant and the steward of clan affairs, appointed by the Lord Lyon, is Clan Commander Colonel George Brown MacGillivray.

## MacGregor Clan Tartan

**EARLIEST KNOWN DATE:**
1810–20
**EARLIEST RECORDED SOURCE:**
Cockburn Collection, 1810–20
**STATUS:**
Certified by the chief, c.1816
**TYPE:**
Symmetrical

A sample of this tartan can be seen in the Cockburn Collection. The same pattern is recorded by Wilson in the 1819 pattern book under the name MacGregor Murray Tartan. Logan (1831) calls it simply MacGregor. It is one of the very few tartans authentically recorded in the *Vestiarium Scoticum*. There is also a certified MacGregor tartan (for undress) called Rob Roy, which is a simple red and black check.

## MacInnes Clan Tartan

**EARLIEST KNOWN DATE:**
1908
**EARLIEST RECORDED SOURCE:**
Adam, 1908
**STATUS:**
Public Register of Arms, Lyon Court, 1960
**TYPE:**
Symmetrical

The Clan MacInnes of the West and the Clan Innes of Moray are two separate clans, but the similarity in the structure of the MacInnes green tartan and the Innes red sett has resulted in the use of both tartans as dress and hunting tartans by both clans. The notes in the archives of the Scottish Tartans Society attribute the design to the "Onich Grocer", with no further explanation. MacInneses are hereditary bowmen to the chief of MacKinnon.

## MacIntyre and Glenorchy Clan Tartan

**EARLIEST KNOWN DATE:**
1850
**EARLIEST RECORDED SOURCE:**
Smith, 1850
**STATUS:**
Recorded
**TYPE:**
Symmetrical

W. and A. Smith called their version of this tartan MacIntyre of Whitehouse. Although it is different from the sett recorded by the Lord Lyon, it is the one most often available today. Before moving to Badenoch to take protection from Clan Chattan, the MacIntyres were listed as followers of Stewart of Appin. It is also known as Glenorchy district tartan.

## MacKay Clan Tartan

**EARLIEST KNOWN DATE:**
1816
**EARLIEST RECORDED SOURCE:**
Logan, 1831
**STATUS:**
Certified by the chief, c.1816
**TYPE:**
Symmetrical

Wilson of Bannockburn recorded the same sett with blue changed to purple in 1819. Logan calls the colour "corbeau", which is a dark shade of green. The pattern is similar to the Gunn tartan in all but colour, suggesting a territorial origin for both. Recently, historians of Scottish dress have tended to stress the geographical sources, rather than the clan associations, of early Highland tartans. A sample was signed and sealed by the chief for the Highland Society of London in 1816.

## MacKenzie Clan Tartan

**EARLIEST KNOWN DATE:**
1778
**EARLIEST RECORDED SOURCE:**
Wilson's pattern book, 1819
**STATUS:**
Public Register of All Arms and Bearings, 1949
**TYPE:**
Symmetrical

The MacKenzie is the regimental tartan of the Seaforth Highlanders, which were raised by MacKenzie, Earl of Seaforth, in 1778. The clan held lands in Ross-shire and around Muir of Ord, but in the 12th century it was removed to Wester Ross (Kintail) by William the Lion. The MacKenzies were joined by the MacRaes, who became their chiefs' bodyguard, and by the MacLennans, who became their hereditary standard bearers. The chiefly line of Kintail died out and the MacKenzies of Cromarty were recognized as chiefs of

the clan. Wilson's 1819 pattern book records various widths and weights of cloth suitable for the different ranks in the regiment. There is a certified sample in the Collection of the Highland Society of London, signed by Mrs MacKenzie of Seaforth, 1816.

## MACKINLAY CLAN TARTAN

**EARLIEST KNOWN DATE:**
(pre-1600) 1906
**EARLIEST RECORDED SOURCE:**
Johnston, 1906
**STATUS:**
Recorded
**TYPE:**
Symmetrical

The MacKinlay tartan could be described as Black Watch with red. It is similar to the early military setts produced by Wilson of Bannockburn for the MacKenzies, the MacLeods and the Gordons, but there is no mention in Wilson's comprehensive pattern books of a MacKinlay tartan. There are, however, grounds for comparing it with the Farquharson, as MacKinlays are named in that clan. To further confuse the issue, the sett is identical to Logan's Murray of Atholl, for which an ancient provenance is claimed.

## MACKINNON CLAN TARTAN

**EARLIEST KNOWN DATE:**
1816
**EARLIEST RECORDED SOURCE:**
Highland Society of London, c.1816
**STATUS:**
Approved, Lyon Court Book, 9 December 1960
**TYPE:**
Symmetrical

The MacKinnon tartan, now generally available and approved by the chief, has altered its appearance over the years, returning to the form of the earliest example.
The collection of certified tartans made by the Highland Society of London, c.1816, includes a specimen signed by the MacKinnon in which the purple stripes are a light shade of azure, a minor change that is mirrored in other tartans, notably the Royal Stewart. Logan (1831) recorded these stripes in white, Smibert (1850) in pink, Smith (1850) in crimson, Mclan (1847) in black and white, and Grant (1886) as black. MacKinnons are associated with the Isle of Iona as early Church leaders. A Gaelic interpretation of the name has been anglicized to "Love".

## MacKintosh Clan Tartan

**EARLIEST KNOWN DATE:**
1815
**EARLIEST RECORDED SOURCE:**
Logan, 1831
**STATUS:**
Lyon Court Book, 1951
**TYPE:**
Symmetrical

D. C. Stewart wrote: "This is one of the few ancient tartans too well authenticated to admit of doubt or question." The earliest publication is attributed to Logan, but he may well have known of the sample, sealed with the signature of the chief, which existed in the Collection of the Highland Society of London, dated around 1816. The chiefs of the MacKintoshes were also chiefs of Clan Chattan. Logan wrote that "the chief also wears a particular tartan of a very showy pattern", which has now been registered with

the Lord Lyon (1947) as "Clan Chattan (Chief)". The clan tartan has likewise been registered as Clan Chattan.

## MacLachlan Clan Tartan

**EARLIEST KNOWN DATE:**
1831
**EARLIEST RECORDED SOURCE:**
Smibert, 1850
**STATUS:**
Recorded
**TYPE:**
Symmetrical

T. Smibert produced a book entitled, *The Clans of the Highlands of Scotland* in 1850 which is widely regarded as an accurate source for the tartans illustrated within it. Smibert had access to the patterns of Wilson of Bannockburn and to the works of Logan and the Sobieski Stuart brothers. Of the three distinct versions of MacLachlan tartan, Smibert's rendering is the one woven today, and it would appear to have a longer history than might be gathered from the date of its first publication.

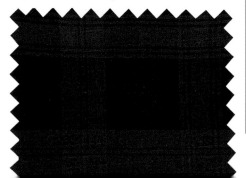

## MacLaine of Lochbuie Clan Tartan

**EARLIEST KNOWN DATE:**
c.1810–20
**EARLIEST RECORDED SOURCE:**
Cockburn Collection, 1810–20
**STATUS:**
Recorded
**TYPE:**
Symmetrical

The MacLaines of Lochbuie are descended from Eachin, the brother of Lachlan, who was the ancestor of the MacLeans of Duart. The chiefship of Clan MacLean (*Clann Gillean*) was settled by tanistry, and Lachlan was recognized as chief. The MacLaines of Lochbuie were followers of the Lords of the Isles and were granted lands on the Isle of Mull. Castle Moy at Loch Buie, now ruined, was the seat of the MacLaines for over 500 years.

## *MacLaine of Lochbuie Hunting Clan Tartan*

**EARLIEST KNOWN DATE:**
1906
**EARLIEST RECORDED SOURCE:**
Johnston, 1906
**STATUS:**
Recorded
**TYPE:**
Symmetrical

The hunting version first appeared in this century, in the work of H. Whyte, published by W. and A. K. Johnston in 1906. This book introduced many new hunting and dress forms of both clan and family tartans. D. W. Stewart (1893) pointed out that the use of so much blue was unique among old tartan setts.

## *MacLaren Clan Tartan*

**EARLIEST KNOWN DATE:**
pre-1820
**EARLIEST RECORDED SOURCE:**
Wilson's pattern book, 1819
**STATUS:**
Approved
**TYPE:**
Symmetrical

The MacLaren differs from the Ferguson of Atholl only in having a yellow line where the latter has a white line. They share the unusual feature of an unbroken band of blue. The present tartan appears under this name in McIan's plate for Clan MacLaren. Wilson was producing it before 1820, but under the name Regent. The Regency ended when George IV succeeded to the throne in 1820, and the name of the tartan became outdated. Production of the sett continued, however, as we know from specimens attached to customers' orders for more.

## *MacLaren Dress Clan Tartan*

**EARLIEST KNOWN DATE:**
1981
**EARLIEST RECORDED SOURCE:**
I. G. Campbell MacLaren, 1981
**STATUS:**
Approved by clan chief, 1981
**TYPE:**
Symmetrical

This sett was approved by the chief and accepted by the Clan MacLaren Society as dress MacLaren in 1981. The sett has been designed by changing the blue ground of the usual MacLaren sett to white and then centring a blue stripe on the white ground. This illustration is taken from a kilt belonging to the designer, I. G. Campbell MacLaren.

## MACLEAN OF DUART CLAN TARTAN

**EARLIEST KNOWN DATE:**
c.1810–20
**EARLIEST RECORDED SOURCE:**
Cockburn Collection, 1810–20
**STATUS:**
Recorded
**TYPE:**
Symmetrical

The pattern is recorded by W. and A. Smith (1850) and by Grant (1886). Logan (1831) gives a variation with a single azure stripe, but the sample in the Cockburn Collection, which is earlier, indicates that, in this instance, Logan was wrong. There is a curious mathematical similarity with the Royal Stewart tartan, in which the number of threads and the colours have been reversed. It suggests there may be a common origin in the designs, but no explanation can be given.

Branches of the clan include the MacLaines of Lochbuie, who broke away after disputing the right of chiefship. Colonel Sir Fitzroy MacLean, 10th baronet and 26th chief, acquired Duart Castle, Isle of Mull, in 1911. He died aged 100, having restored the family seat to its former glory. There is also a hunting MacLean tartan of a different design.

## MACLEOD CLAN TARTAN

**EARLIEST KNOWN DATE:**
(1777) 1831
**EARLIEST RECORDED SOURCE:**
Logan, 1831
**STATUS:**
Approved by the chief, 1910
**TYPE:**
Symmetrical

This sett has its source in the MacKenzie tartan used in 1777 by John MacKenzie, called Lord MacLeod, when he raised a regiment called Lord MacLeod's Highlanders. The family claimed to be heirs of Roderick, the last chief of Lewis, who had died in 1595. This tartan was approved by Chief Norman Magnus, 26th chief, in 1910, and has been the usual modern sett since then. There is also a yellow dress MacLeod, which was first published in the *Vestiarium Scoticum* but which may have been designed some years earlier. The present chief, John MacLeod, lives in Dunvegan Castle, Skye.

## MACLEOD RED CLAN TARTAN

**EARLIEST KNOWN DATE:**
(1747) 1982
**EARLIEST RECORDED SOURCE:**
Design: Ruairidh MacLeod, 1982
**STATUS:**
Approved, 1982
**TYPE:**
Symmetrical

The design of this tartan was based on the one worn by Norman MacLeod, 22nd chief of the clan, in a portrait by Allan Ramsay (1713–84) in 1748. In accordance with normal contemporary practice, the costume was painted for Ramsay by Van Haecken, using an 11-yard (10-metre) bolt of tartan specially ordered from Skye by MacLeod in 1747. To enhance the family resemblance to other MacLeod tartans and to differentiate this from Murray of Tullibardine, the name now attached to the sett in the portrait, Ruairidh MacLeod added a yellow stripe to the sett.

## MACMILLAN ANCIENT CLAN TARTAN

**EARLIEST KNOWN DATE:**
1847
**EARLIEST RECORDED SOURCE:**
Cant after Mclan (1847)
**STATUS:**
Recorded
**TYPE:**
Asymmetrical

The term "ancient" is normally used to describe a lighter choice of colour tones that can be applied to any tartan. In the case of MacMillan the "ancient" form involves a more radical change, justifying the traditional use of the adjective in the name of the tartan. Logan (1847) stated that this version is identical with Buchanan. The thread count was deduced by Cant from the illustration by Mclan in *The Clans of the Scottish Highlands*. In 1951 Lieutenant General Sir Gordon MacMillan was recognized as chief of the clan by the Lord Lyon.

## MACNAB CLAN TARTAN

**EARLIEST KNOWN DATE:**
c.1816
**EARLIEST RECORDED SOURCE:**
Logan, 1831
**STATUS:**
Certified by the McNabb, c.1816
**TYPE:**
Symmetrical

The structure of the MacNab is identical with that of the Black Watch, but, by a translation of colours, the most subdued of tartans becomes one of the most striking.

D. C. Stewart (1950) suggested that the pattern should be looked at through a green filter to see the effect. James Charles MacNab of MacNab, Wester Kilmany, Fife, was recognized as chief in 1970.

## MacNaughton Clan Tartan

**EARLIEST KNOWN DATE:**
1831
**EARLIEST RECORDED SOURCE:**
Logan, 1831
**STATUS:**
Recorded
**TYPE:**
Symmetrical

The MacNaughton tartan is also recorded by W. and A. Smith in the *Authenticated Tartans of the Clans and Families of Scotland* (1850). Other works omit the narrow black stripe, leaving a single plain band of azure, but this is generally regarded as an error. The tartan resembles the MacDuff. The present chief is Sir Patrick MacNaughten of MacNaughten. The tartan is worn by the Vale of Atholl pipe band.

## MacNeil Clan Tartan

**EARLIEST KNOWN DATE:**
1819
**EARLIEST RECORDED SOURCE:**
Grant, 1886
**STATUS:**
Recorded
**TYPE:**
Symmetrical

This version with the narrow guards about the yellow stripe is the usual modern form. It differs from Logan's 1831 version which had broad dark lines in place of the narrow ones. The MacNeils claim descent from Niall, King of Ireland, who came to Barra in 1049. They are the hereditary pipers to the MacLeans of Duart. The present chief, Professor Ian Roderick MacNeil of Barra, lives in Chicago, USA. The MacNeil tartan is distinguished from the Campbell of Argyll by having the white stripe on the blue rather than the green.

## MacNeil of Colonsay Clan Tartan

**EARLIEST KNOWN DATE:**
*c.*1819
**EARLIEST RECORDED SOURCE:**
Johnston, 1906, and various authors
**STATUS:**
Recorded
**TYPE:**
Symmetrical

MacNeil tartans had been produced by Wilson since 1819. Wilson made various changes to the MacNeil sett over the years and it appears that Johnston's Colonsay version is based on those earlier examples. It is certainly quite different from the certified specimen in the collection of the Highland Society of London (*c.*1816), which is much closer to the MacDonald or the Glengarry tartans. MacNeils of Colonsay are a branch of the Clan MacNeil.

## MacPhee Clan Tartan

**EARLIEST KNOWN DATE:**
1906
**EARLIEST RECORDED SOURCE:**
Johnston, 1906
**STATUS:**
Lyon Court Book, 1991
**TYPE:**
Symmetrical

This tartan was registered by the Lord Lyon on 29 August 1991 and approved by the chief. The chief also approved a black and white MacPhee. MacPhee, MacFie or MacDuffie held lands on the Isle of Colonsay until the mid-17th century but were later scattered by the clearances. They were the hereditary keeper of the records to the Lords of the Isles. The present chief, Sandy MacPhie, lives in Queensland, Australia.

## MacPherson Clan Tartan

**EARLIEST KNOWN DATE:**
1819
**EARLIEST RECORDED SOURCE:**
Grant, 1886
**STATUS:**
Certified by the chief, c.1816
**TYPE:**
Symmetrical

Wilson produced a version he called "No. 43, Kidd and Caledonian", before it became MacPherson in 1822. James Grant took all 72 of the tartans in his book from actual specimens in use at the time (1886), and his version more closely matches the tartan in use today. Grant's version has a slight reduction in the red ground. MacPherson of Cluny certified the sample in the Collection of the Highland Society of London (c.1816).

## MacQuarrie Clan Tartan

**EARLIEST KNOWN DATE:**
1815
**EARLIEST RECORDED SOURCE:**
Grant, 1886
**STATUS:**
Certified by the chief, c.1816
**TYPE:**
Symmetrical

There are many variations of the MacQuarrie sett. The version in use today was first illustrated by Grant (1886), but the earliest version is a sample in the Cockburn Collection (c.1815). D. C. Stewart wrote: "The MacQuarrie tartan now most often used is related to the red MacDonald." The MacQuarries claim descent from the Clan Alpin, who had territory on the Isles of Mull and Ulva and were followers of the Lords of the Isles. The chiefship is vacant at present.

## MACQUEEN CLAN TARTAN

**EARLIEST KNOWN DATE:**
1842
**EARLIEST RECORDED SOURCE:**
*Vestiarium Scoticum,* 1842
**STATUS:**
Recorded
**TYPE:**
Symmetrical

This is the tartan of the Clan Revan, so called after Revan MacMulmor MacAngus MacQueen, who led kinsmen of the MacDonald bride for the 10th chief of the MacKintoshes to take protection from Clan Chattan. As far as is known, the sett was unnamed before the publication in the *Vestiarium Scoticum* (1842), but this source is unreliable. It has much in common with the Fraser and the Gunn tartans, both of which have four bold stripes.

## MACRAE CLAN TARTAN

**EARLIEST KNOWN DATE:**
1850
**EARLIEST RECORDED SOURCE:**
Smith, 1850
**STATUS:**
Recorded
**TYPE:**
Symmetrical

This pattern is taken from the manuscript of the Smiths' *Authenticated Tartans of the Clans and Families of Scotland,* and a minor error in the count was corrected by D. C. Stewart (1950). The Smiths' sources included the findings of George Hunter, who toured the Highlands in search of old tartans prior to 1822. A different tartan, The Prince's Own, exists in the Collection of the Highland Society of London (*c.*1816). Eilean Donan Castle on the Kyle of Lochalsh was the stronghold of the MacRaes, who were Constables for the earls of Seaforth.

## MALCOLM CLAN TARTAN

**EARLIEST KNOWN DATE:**
(1847) 1850
**EARLIEST RECORDED SOURCE:**
Smith, 1850
**STATUS:**
Recorded
**TYPE:**
Asymmetrical

The name Malcolm, as distinct from MacCallum, was established in 1770 when the 9th chief of Poltalloch changed the family name to Malcolm. This may well be the sett on which the MacCallum was based "from the recollection of old people in Argyllshire" and that D. W. Stewart illustrated in silk in his book (1893).
Wilson of Bannockburn produced a symmetrical version of the Malcolm tartan, which was recorded in the firm's 1847 pattern book. The gold and azure of the additional stripes can be found in the armorial bearings of the Malcolm family.

## MATHESON CLAN TARTAN

**EARLIEST KNOWN DATE:**
1850
**EARLIEST RECORDED SOURCE:**
Smith, 1850
**STATUS:**
Recorded
**TYPE:**
Symmetrical

The design usually worn by Mathesons is given by W. and A. Smith, although earlier versions are recorded. Mclan's *c.*1845 drawing could be taken to represent either of the two red designs of which this is one. The Mathesons were involved with other clans like the MacDonells of Glengarry and the MacKenzies of Kintail. The tartan has a design structure that relates to the Glengarry, which dates at least to *c.*1816, when a sample was certified by the chief.

## MAXWELL CLAN TARTAN

**EARLIEST KNOWN DATE:**
1842
**EARLIEST RECORDED SOURCE:**
*Vestiarium Scoticum*, 1842
**STATUS:**
Recorded
**TYPE:**
Symmetrical

Tartans of the Lowland families were not named until the publication the *Vestiarium Scoticum* in 1842. The authors, the Sobieski Stuart brothers, enjoyed a popular following among the Scottish gentry in the early Victorian era, and, in the spirit of the times, added mystery, romance and some spurious historical documentation to the subject of tartans. The Maxwells have, nevertheless, a tartan at least 150 years old and probably designed by persons of great imagination and flair.

## MENZIES HUNTING CLAN TARTAN

**EARLIEST KNOWN DATE:**
1815
**EARLIEST RECORDED SOURCE:**
Stewart, 1893
**STATUS:**
Highland Society of London, *c.*1816
**TYPE:**
Symmetrical

This sett is woven in various colours — black, green and red — with the same basic design. The sample in the Cockburn Collection is labelled "McFarlane" in General Cockburn's own handwriting. He carried out this task in 1815, when information about the names of tartans could only be found by personal research. The certified version in the collection of the Highland Society of London is red. D. W. Stewart's book shows the green "hunting" version, woven in silk.

## *MONCREIFFE (MACLACHLAN)*
## *CLAN TARTAN*

**EARLIEST KNOWN DATE:**
1819
**EARLIEST RECORDED SOURCE:**
Wilson's pattern book, 1819
**STATUS:**
Lyon Court Book, 1978
**TYPE:**
Equal check

Sir Iain Moncreiffe of that Ilk acquired the MacLachlan old sett for the clan when he became chief in 1957. Micheil MacDonald (1991) wrote: "As a result of a long association with Clan Murray, the Moncreiffes traditionally wore the Atholl tartan. Bur Sir Iain . . . arranged that Madam MacLachlan of MacLachlan assign to him a 'primitive' pattern of red and green squares."

## *MONTGOMERIE FAMILY*
## *TARTAN*

**EARLIEST KNOWN DATE:**
1893
**EARLIEST RECORDED SOURCE:**
Stewart, 1893
**STATUS:**
Recorded
**TYPE:**
Symmetrical

D. W. Stewart was of the opinion that this sett could be traced back to 1707, when it was adopted by the Montgomeries, earls of Eglinton. The Eglinton district sett has a reduced proportion of the purple ground colour. There is a completely different pattern in the Collection of the Highland Society of London.

## *MORRISON CLAN TARTAN*

**EARLIEST KNOWN DATE:**
1747
**EARLIEST RECORDED SOURCE:**
Lyon Court Book, 1968
**STATUS:**
Approved
**TYPE:**
Symmetrical

Discovered in a Morrison family bible, the sett dates from 1747. The Lord Lyon wrote that it showed "the most authentic existing pattern of what the Morrisons wore in those days", and based the new tartan on the relic.

## MUIR CLAN TARTAN

**EARLIEST KNOWN DATE:**
(1880) 1930
**EARLIEST RECORDED SOURCE:**
Ross, 1930
**STATUS:**
Recorded
**TYPE:**
Symmetrical

The Muir tartan has the traditional blue–black–green base, but with an unusual motif of three narrow red stripes appearing twice on the green square. A similar device is seen in the Cochrane tartan. At about the same time that the tartan was documented by Ross, it was being woven by Anderson in Edinburgh from a pattern that the firm believed to be about 50 years old. The Muirs of More held lands in Ayrshire.

## MUNRO CLAN TARTAN

**EARLIEST KNOWN DATE:**
c.1810–20
**EARLIEST RECORDED SOURCE:**
Cockburn Collection, 1810–20
**STATUS:**
Recorded
**TYPE:**
Symmetrical

This sett is usually regarded as the correct form of the Munro tartan. It is illustrated by Smibert and the Smith brothers (both 1850). In early versions bright pink replaces the crimson between the three green lines. Munros wear the Black Watch as a hunting tartan.

## MURRAY OF ATHOLL CLAN TARTAN

**EARLIEST KNOWN DATE:**
c.1810–20
**EARLIEST RECORDED SOURCE:**
Cockburn Collection, 1810–20
**STATUS:**
Authorized
**TYPE:**
Symmetrical

This is also known as Atholl district tartan. This sett may have been referred to as early as 1618, when Sir Robert Gordon of Gordonstoun, the tutor of Sutherland, wrote to Murray of Pulrossie, "requesting him to furl his pennon when the Earl of Sutherland's banner was displayed and to remove the red and white lines from the plaids of his men so as to bring their dress into harmony with that of the other septs". Murrays and Sutherlands were of similar origin. The de Moravia tribe from which both descend may have worn the basic sett in the 12th and 13th centuries.

## MURRAY OF TULLIBARDINE CLAN TARTAN

**EARLIEST KNOWN DATE:**
(1679) 1850
**EARLIEST RECORDED SOURCE:**
Smith, 1850
**STATUS:**
Recorded
**TYPE:**
Symmetrical

James Grant (1886) wrote: "That tartan called the Tullibardine is a red tartan, and was adopted and worn by Charles, the first Earl of Dunmore, second son of the first Marquis of Tullibardine . . . in 1679 [he] was lieutenant colonel of the Royal Grey Dragoons." The same sett is shown in the earlier work by the Smith brothers (1850). This is the sett shown in Allan Ramsay's famous 1748 portrait of the chief of the MacLeods, Norman MacLeod, at Dunvegan Castle. (See MacLeod Red, page 60.)

## NICHOLSON MACNICOL CLAN TARTAN

**EARLIEST KNOWN DATE:**
c.1845–7
**EARLIEST RECORDED SOURCE:**
Stewart, 1950, after McIan
**STATUS:**
Recorded
**TYPE:**
Symmetrical

D. C. Stewart wrote of the MacNicol tartan: "Cloth has been woven purporting to show the correct sett, but the sett seems intended for that appearing in McIan's drawing, where no such claim is made for it. The drawing admits of many interpretations; the sett given here is one such reconstruction. The illustrated tartan follows Stewart's reconstruction. In 1980 the Nicholsons and the MacNicols became separate clans. When Lord Carnock was recognized as chief of the Nicholsons, the Lord Lyon accepted a petition from Ian Nicholson of Scorrybreac, chief of the Nicholsons on the Isle of Skye, to change his name and rematriculate his arms as "Iain MacNeacail of MacNeacail and Scorrybreac". Thus the Skye MacNicols are now members of Clan MacNeacail.

## NISBET FAMILY TARTAN

**EARLIEST KNOWN DATE:**
1842
**EARLIEST RECORDED SOURCE:**
Nesbitt, 1941
**STATUS:**
Recorded
**TYPE:**
Symmetrical

This is the sett that appears in the *Vestiarium Scoticum* (1842) under the title of MacKintosh, but that clan has never accepted the pattern. There is no historic connection between the names to explain the position and it is interesting to note the similarity with the Dunbar tartan, which also originates in the *Vestiarium*. The Nisbets came from the old barony of Nisbet in the parish of Edrom, Berwickshire, as early as 1160.

## OGILVIE CLAN TARTAN

**EARLIEST KNOWN DATE:**
1794
**EARLIEST RECORDED SOURCE:**
Smibert, 1850
**STATUS:**
Certified by the chief, 1816
**TYPE:**
Symmetrical

The most complex of all tartans. An early version, recorded by James Logan in 1831, had over 90 colour changes. The resulting pattern was too large for the looms and the yarn used for kilt making at the time. It seems likely that weavers, over the years, have reduced the sett to accommodate these technical limitations. One such sett is illustrated here. It is a simplified version of the Ogilvy of Airly tartan, which was certified by the chief in 1816. The Ogilvie name became connected with the Drummonds of Strathallan in 1812 by a marriage between the two families, and it is only since then that the Drummond sett became known as Ogilvie.

## HUNTING OGILVIE TARTAN

**EARLIEST KNOWN DATE:**
*c.*1829
**EARLIEST RECORDED SOURCE:**
*Vestiarium Scoticum,* 1842
**STATUS:**
Recorded
**TYPE:**
Symmetrical

Wilson of Bannockburn were producing this tartan under the name Inverarity prior to the publication of the *Vestiarium* in 1842, where it is called "Ogilvy of Inverquharity". However, it seems likely that Wilson acquired the pattern from the authors of that book while it was still in preparation, as early as 1829.

## RAMSAY CLAN TARTAN

**EARLIEST KNOWN DATE:**
1842
**EARLIEST RECORDED SOURCE:**
*Vestiarium Scoticum,* 1842
**STATUS:**
Recorded
**TYPE:**
Symmetrical

Ramsay was one of the names adopted by members of the Clan MacGregor when their own was proscribed. It is not surprising, therefore, that an early MacGregor sett was used as a basis for the Ramsay tartan. The *Vestiarium Scoticum* contains a curious mixture of fact and fiction and it is possible that the tartan was in existence long before the earliest recorded date given.

## ROBERTSON CLAN TARTAN

**EARLIEST KNOWN DATE:**
1831
**EARLIEST RECORDED SOURCE:**
Logan, 1831
**STATUS:**
Recorded
**TYPE:**
Symmetrical

The oldest records show the Robertson tartan with a white line, but the modern weavers' sett, without the white, can be traced to Logan's 1831 book. D. C. Stewart noted a subtle difference in Logan's count, which is not reproduced here — namely, the use of contrasting narrow stripes next to the broader stripe. In other words, a narrow green next to the broad blue and a narrow blue next to the broad green. This version, the usual modern form, has blue for all the narrow stripes. Stewart reckoned that it added "balance in the design". Mid-toned blues and greens are used in this illustration.

## ROBERTSON OF KINDEACE CLAN TARTAN

**EARLIEST KNOWN DATE:**
*c.*1810–20
**EARLIEST RECORDED SOURCE:**
Cockburn Collection, 1810–20
**STATUS:**
Recorded
**TYPE:**
Symmetrical

This tartan is also known as the Hunting Robertson. The sett, which is reputedly ancient, resembles the Atholl Murray, although it was used by only the Robertsons from the north. The Robertsons' Kindeace estates are near Tain on the eastern shores of the northern Highlands, north of Inverness.

## ROSE CLAN TARTAN

**EARLIEST KNOWN DATE:**
1842
**EARLIEST RECORDED SOURCE:**
*Vestiarium Scoticum,* 1842
**STATUS:**
Public Register of All Arms and Bearings, 1946
**TYPE:**
Symmetrical

The text of the *Vestiarium* gives the colours as purple and crimson, but in the plate they appear as mid-blue and scarlet. The Lord Lyon records crimson as red. D. C. Stewart (1950) regarded this sett as a dress tartan, although James Logan recorded a hunting version in 1831. The Castle of Kilravock near Inverness is the seat of the chief.

## ROSS CLAN TARTAN

**EARLIEST KNOWN DATE:**
c.1810–20
**EARLIEST RECORDED SOURCE:**
Cockburn Collection, 1810–20
**STATUS:**
Recorded
**TYPE:**
Symmetrical

The oldest version of the Ross tartan, that in the Cockburn Collection, is the one in use today. Later versions, including Logan's, are known to have omissions. The Clan Ross is descended from Fearcher MacinTagart, Earl of Ross in the 13th century. The chiefship has passed to the Rosses of Shandwick. The tartan is also worn by the MacTiers.

## SCOTT CLAN/FAMILY TARTAN

**EARLIEST KNOWN DATE:**
Unknown
**EARLIEST RECORDED SOURCE:**
MacKinlay, 1930–50
**STATUS:**
Recorded
**TYPE:**
Symmetrical

Also known as Red Scott, this tartan is generally available today. The Chief of the Scotts is His Grace the 9th Duke of Buccleuch and 10th of Queensberry, who lives in Selkirk in the Borders region of Scotland. Sir Walter Scott was of the opinion that Lowland families had no clan tartan tradition except for various patterns of the Shepherd's Plaid. Black and white check is often a feature of Lowland and Border clan tartans produced today. The MacKinlay Collection of tartans and related material is kept at the Scottish Tartans Society in Comrie, Perthshire.

# The Tartans of the Clan Shaw

The Shaw tartan was first published in a drawing by McIan of Fearcher Shaw of the Black Watch, who was executed for mutiny in 1743, which appeared in *The Clans of the Scottish Highlands* (1845–7). Co-author, James Logan, describes the figure as wearing the Regimental tartan with a red line to distinguish the philabeg from the belted plaid. Regimental is another name for the Government or Black Watch tartan. The Shaw tartan has two, almost-imperceptible, black lines in the border of the blue square. It appears that McIan drew these lines intending that his assistants would "colour in" the space between, but this was never done. McIan, of course, did not name the tartan, but in those early Victorian days, such was the passion for all things Scottish, that the graphical error in the rendering of the "Black Watch" was taken to be the previously unknown "Shaw" tartan. For this reason John Shaw of Tordarroch, 22nd chief, had a new Shaw tartan designed reflecting the genuine historical connections with the Clan MacKintosh and Clan Chattan. He wrote, "The Lyon recognition of the more recent design is specifically without prejudice to the continued use of the hitherto accepted Shaw tartan."

## SHAW CLAN TARTAN

**EARLIEST KNOWN DATE:**
1845
**EARLIEST RECORDED SOURCE:**
McIan, *c.* 1845–7
**STATUS:**
Approved
**TYPE:**
Symmetrical

The Shaw tartan, it appears, had been derived from errors in the graphic illustration of the Black Watch. For this reason, John Shaw of Tordarroch, 22nd chief, had a new Shaw tartan designed to reflect the genuine historical connections with Clan Mackintosh and Clan Chattan. He wrote in 1971, in correspondence to the Scottish Tartans Society: "The Lyon recognition of the more recent design is specifically without prejudice to the continued use of the hitherto accepted Shaw tartan."

## SHAW OF TORDARROCH
## CLAN TARTAN

**EARLIEST KNOWN DATE:**
1969
**EARLIEST RECORDED SOURCE:**
Design: D. C. Stewart, 1971
**STATUS:**
Lyon Court Book, 1971
**TYPE:**
Symmetrical

When Major C. J. Shaw of Tordarroch matriculated and became the first chief of the clan for some 400 years, he had a new tartan designed to reflect the clan's MacKintosh ancestry. He specifically states that the old design is, however, still perfectly acceptable and approves its continued use by all members of the clan.

## SINCLAIR CLAN TARTAN

**EARLIEST KNOWN DATE:**
1810–20
**EARLIEST RECORDED SOURCE:**
Logan, 1831
**STATUS:**
Lyon Court Book, 1951
**TYPE:**
Symmetrical

The Lord Lyon recorded the Sinclair in its smallest proportions, but the sett can be multiplied at the discretion of the weaver. This is a minor variation on the specimen in the Cockburn Collection, which also appears in a painting of Alexander, 13th Earl of Caithness (1790–1858). The present chief is Malcolm Sinclair, 20th Earl of Sinclair.

## SKENE CLAN TARTAN

**EARLIEST KNOWN DATE:**
1830
**EARLIEST RECORDED SOURCE:**
Grant, 1886
**STATUS:**
Recorded
**TYPE:**
Symmetrical

Grant's version is similar to the sample named Skene in Wilson's 1830 pattern book, although Logan had included this sett in *The Scottish Gael* (1831) under the name of Logan. There is a similarity in design to the Robertson tartan, which corresponds to the tradition that Skenes were descended from the Robertsons of Atholl.

# The Tartans of Clan Stewart

The Royal House of Stewart dates from the 12th century, when King David I appointed Walter Fitz Alan as High Steward of Scotland. Walter's stewardship was made a hereditary title and in time the family became known as Stewart. Robert the Bruce's grandson, Robert II (1371–90), was the first Stewart to become king. The main branches of the clan have a common ancestor in Sir John of Bonkyl (d.1298). He had seven sons whose descendants became the Earls of Angus, Lennox, Galloway, Buchan and Traquair, as well as the Lords of Lorne and Innermeath. Since the demise of the Lennox branch, the Stewarts of Galloway now represent the senior line of the family. The best known of the Stewart tartans are those of the Stewarts of Appin and Ardsheil, the Stewarts of Atholl, and the Stuarts of Bute. The Royal Stewart tartan, possibly the best known of all Scottish tartans, was worn by King George IV during his state visit to Edinburgh in 1822, and was later adopted by King George V for the House of Windsor to mark the ancient link to the Royal House of Stewart. This came from George of Hanover (crowned in 1714), who was the great grandson of James VI and I, the Stewart King of Scotland and England (1603). George V is reputed to have said that his adopted tartan could be worn by all the members of his family, which at the time was taken to mean all the peoples of the British Empire!

## ROYAL STEWART ROYAL FAMILY TARTAN

**EARLIEST KNOWN DATE:**
c.1800
**EARLIEST RECORDED SOURCE:**
Logan, 1831
**STATUS:**
Approved by George V
**TYPE:**
Symmetrical

The best known of all Scottish tartans, the Royal Stewart is the tartan of the Royal House of Stewart and the personal tartan of Her Majesty the Queen. In the same way that clansmen wear the tartan of their chief, it is appropriate for all subjects of the Queen to wear the Royal Stewart tartan. References indicate that the sett was known at the end of the 18th century. Early samples show the blue as a light azure.

### STEWART OF APPIN CLAN TARTAN

**EARLIEST KNOWN DATE:**
1820
**EARLIEST RECORDED SOURCE:**
John Cargill, 1950
**STATUS:**
Recorded
**TYPE:**
Symmetrical

Stewarts of Appin feuded relentlessly with the Campbells, supported by some of the Clan MacColl, whose tartan is clearly based on the Appin. Unlike the other Stewart tartans, Appin is more akin to the MacKintosh group of tartans. Drawings of a different sett, which mimicked the Royal Stewart, were prepared for, but not included in, the *Vestiarium Scoticum*. Stewarts of Ardsheil, a branch of the Appin clan, have their own certified tartan, which, by its similarity and early provenance, supports the authenticity of this version of the Appin.

### STEWART DRESS CLAN TARTAN

**EARLIEST KNOWN DATE:**
19th century
**EARLIEST RECORDED SOURCE:**
Not attributed
**STATUS:**
Recorded
**TYPE:**
Symmetrical

The dress version of James Logan's Royal Stewart was compared by D. C. Stewart to a 200-year-old silk scarf with the remark that "the design had been well maintained". In this pattern the blue is joined to the black and the yellow and white are of equal size. The red stripe on the white, not present here, signifies a "Victoria" sett. The Dress Stewart tartan alongside its formal partner, the Royal Stewart, is known throughout the world as a symbol of Scotland.

### STEWART OF ATHOLL CLAN TARTAN

**EARLIEST KNOWN DATE:**
(1745), pre-1842
**EARLIEST RECORDED SOURCE:**
*Vestiarium Scoticum*, 1842
**STATUS:**
Recorded
**TYPE:**
Symmetrical

This design was prepared for the *Vestiarium Scoticum* but not included in the published version. It was claimed to be the sett of a "relic from the '45" and published as such by D. W. Stewart in 1893. It has become more widely known in recent times.

## HUNTING STEWART GENERAL TARTAN

**EARLIEST KNOWN DATE:**
1819
**EARLIEST RECORDED SOURCE:**
Wilson's pattern book, 1819
**STATUS:**
Recorded
**TYPE:**
Asymmetrical

The pattern books of Wilson of Bannockburn provide the first record of this sett, but the pattern was not published until 1886, when James Grant included it in *The Tartans of the Clans of Scotland*. Grant's version has an extra black line. The pattern is unusual in that the half sett is not reversed to create a symmetrical square. Instead the full sett is simply repeated from right to left across the cloth. There is no reliable explanation why Hunting Stewart should be regarded as a general tartan other than, perhaps, that hunting tartans are not formal wear and not therefore subject to the rigours of clan protocol. Black Watch, an equally suitable choice for a hunting tartan, is worn without regard to clan affiliation.

---

## OLD STEWART CLAN TARTAN

**EARLIEST KNOWN DATE:**
1819
**EARLIEST RECORDED SOURCE:**
Wilson's pattern book, 1819
**STATUS:**
Recorded
**TYPE:**
Symmetrical

A sample of this sett is included in the Royal Tartans collection at the Scottish Tartans Society under the title Stewart of Bute, but it is often regarded as the clan tartan as distinct from the Royal Stewart. Captain Stuart Davidson, founder chairman of the Scottish Tartans Society, suggested that it belonged to the Stewarts of the Western Isles. The Stuarts of Bute have a distinct tartan of their own, but of a later date.

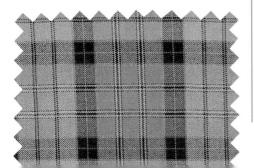

## PRINCE CHARLES EDWARD TARTAN

**EARLIEST KNOWN DATE:**
*c.* 1810–20
**EARLIEST RECORDED SOURCE:**
Cockburn Collection, 1810–20
**STATUS:**
Recorded
**TYPE:**
Symmetrical

This tartan is also known as the Earl of Moray. A very similar piece exists in the Collection of the Highland Society of London (*c.* 1815) in which the yellow and white are in silk. This sett is identical with the Royal Stewart apart from the much reduced red square. D. C. Stewart wrote: "the tartan becomes richer to the point of congestion." It is reputed to have been worn by the prince when he was at Holyrood in 1745–6.

## STUART OF BUTE CLAN TARTAN

**EARLIEST KNOWN DATE:**
1842
**EARLIEST RECORDED SOURCE:**
*Vestiarium Scoticum,* 1842
**STATUS:**
Approved
**TYPE:**
Symmetrical

The use of this tartan is normally considered to be confined to the family from whom it derives its title, although other, more or less closely related families, have likewise claimed an interest. Whether the pattern was in use before the publication of the *Vestiarium Scoticum* has never been ascertained. It is often seen in maroon, but the change from red does not have the approval of the Marquis of Bute. Stewart and Stuart are different spellings of the same name. Some families, including the Stuarts of Bute, have adopted the French spelling, introduced by Mary, Queen of Scots.

## SUTHERLAND CLAN TARTAN

**EARLIEST KNOWN DATE:**
(1618), 1842
**EARLIEST RECORDED SOURCE:**
*Vestiarium Scoticum,* 1842
**STATUS:**
Recorded
**TYPE:**
Symmetrical

The earlier date refers to a letter from Sir Robert Gordon, tutor of Sutherland, instructing Murray of Pulrossie to "remove the red and white lines from the plaids of the men so as to bring their dress into harmony with that of the other Septs". The Old Sutherland tartan shown here with its red and white stripes must theoretically, therefore, pre-date this instruction. The sett was also recorded by Smibert (1850). The "new" Sutherland is the same as the Black Watch, which is worn by the Argyll and Sutherland Highlanders with the material kilted (folded) to show the green.

## TEALL OF TEALLACH

**EARLIEST KNOWN DATE:**
1966
**EARLIEST RECORDED SOURCE:**
Designed by D. C. Dalgliesh, 1966
**STATUS:**
Accredited by Scottish Tartans Society, 1966
**TYPE:**
Symmetrical, reproduction colours

The Teall tartan was designed to include the historical connections of the Teall family by the weaving manufacturer D. C. Dalgliesh and accredited by the Scottish Tartans Society in 1966. Teall of Teallach (Pitlochry, Perthshire) is associated with the House of Gordon, hence the yellow stripe; the Singer Sewing Machine Company, hence the red; the merchant navy, hence the blue; and the Priory Independent Schools, hence the black. White forms part of the Teallach coat of arms. The tartan has been adopted by the Tartan Society in Scotland and the town of Highlands, North Carolina, USA, where the Scottish Tartans Museum in America was founded. The head of the family is Dr Gordon Teall of Teallach who is the present (1993) chairman of the Society.

## URQUHART CLAN TARTAN

**EARLIEST KNOWN DATE:**
c. 1810–20
**EARLIEST RECORDED SOURCE:**
Cockburn Collection, 1810–20
**STATUS:**
Lyon Court Book, 1991
**TYPE:**
Symmetrical

The Urquhart tartan was registered in 1991, by the chief, Kenneth Tryst Urquhart of Urquhart. The Lord Lyon also registered the Urquhart White Line which can be regarded as a dress version. The proportions of the Cockburn Collection sample show a slightly broader red stripe, known today as the Urquhart Broad Red.

## WALLACE CLAN TARTAN

**EARLIEST KNOWN DATE:**
1842
**EARLIEST RECORDED SOURCE:**
*Vestiarium Scoticum,* 1842
**STATUS:**
Recorded
**TYPE:**
Symmetrical

D. C. Stewart wrote that the tartan "was known from examples in early collections of specimens", a phrase he generally used to indicate the Collection of the Highland Society of London, but in this instance the author can find no trace. The present chief is Lt. Col. M. R. Wallace of that Ilk.

## WEMYSS CLAN TARTAN

**EARLIEST KNOWN DATE:**
1842
**EARLIEST RECORDED SOURCE:**
*Vestiarium Scoticum*, 1842
**STATUS:**
Recorded
**TYPE:**
Symmetrical

The name derives phonetically from the Gaelic word for "cave", and probably refers to the caves below MacDuff's Castle at Easter Wemyss, near Kirkcaldy, Fife. There is an interesting article on the family of Wemyss in William Anderson's book *The Scottish Nation,* published in 1874.

## WOTHERSPOON FAMILY TARTAN

**EARLIEST KNOWN DATE:**
*c.*1941
**EARLIEST RECORDED SOURCE:**
William Anderson, Edinburgh, 1947
**STATUS:**
Recorded
**TYPE:**
Symmetrical

This sett comes from the MacGregor-Hastie collection. It was obtained from Anderson of Edinburgh in 1947. Wotherspoons are recorded in the Lowlands of Scotland from the beginning of the 14th century. The Rev. John Witherspoon (1722—94), born in Yester, East Lothian, was president of Princeton University in 1768 and took an active part in the American Revolution.

## YOUNG FAMILY TARTAN

**EARLIEST KNOWN DATE:**
1991
**EARLIEST RECORDED SOURCE:**
Design: Lochcarron Weavers
**STATUS:**
Accredited by Scottish Tartans Society, 1992
**TYPE:**
Symmetrical

This tartan is based on the Christina Young arisaid, which dates from 1726 and is preserved at the Scottish Tartans Museum in Comrie, Perthshire. It is one of the oldest and most complete preserved specimens of homespun handloom weaving in existence. The blue and green background colours are normally woven at twice the width shown here for a kilt tartan. The design retains the unusual purple—yellow—orange box check of the original blanket and changes only the ground colour to the traditional west coast greens and blues.

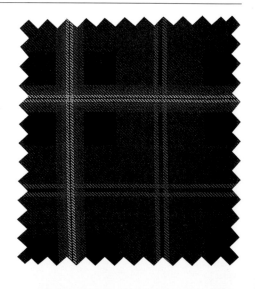

# GLOSSARY

**ARISAID:** a blanket or shawl.

**BADGE:** the clan badge is the heraldic crest of the chief surrounded by a strap and buckle which may be worn by the clansmen.

**BEG:** small (Gaelic).

**BLACK WATCH:** nickname applied to the Independent Companies c.1700 who kept watch on the activities of the Jacobite clans (black meaning secret or undercover) and later (1739) the 43rd Regiment.

**CADET:** a family descended from the younger sons or daughters of an earlier chief.

**DRESS TARTAN:** a tartan in which one of the background colours has been changed to white. Used in kilts for Highland dancing.

**FENCIBLE REGIMENTS:** companies of regular troops on horse and foot, raised for home service in 1759, 1778–9 and 1794 for special emergencies. The word is short for "defensible".

**FEU:** rent.

**GUARDS:** a design element in tartan where black lines on either side of a narrow stripe give added definition.

**HARD TARTAN:** very fine but densely woven, coarse wool tartan produced until the mid-19th century.

**HUNTING TARTAN:** green or subdued tartan for informal or everyday wear.

**ILK:** same place, as in "of that Ilk", where a person's name is the same as the name of his or her territorial designation.

**JACOBITE:** of King James VII and II (deposed in 1689), a Stewart loyalist.

**LORD LYON:** an officer of the crown, presiding over the Lyon Court, in matters of heraldry and succession in Scotland.

**OVERCHECK:** a narrow stripe superimposed on the structure of a tartan design.

**PHILABEG:** kilt. A length of single width tartan cloth with fixed pleats.

**SEPT:** clan, but often used to mean a part or branch of a clan. Many clansmen were known by a surname in addition to their clan name: for example the MacIans of Clan Donald. The term is also applied to unrelated families who take protection from the clan.

**SETT:** another word for pattern which is used to describe the area of the design that is repeated.

**TANISTRY:** the heir apparent to a Celtic chief chosen by election during the chief's lifetime.

**THREAD:** spun woollen yarn of a single colour.

**THREAD COUNT:** the number of threads of each of the sequence of colours of the sett.

**TRAMLINES:** double black lines seen in many of the Black Watch-based tartans.

**UNDRESS:** informal.

# REFERENCES AND FURTHER READING

Some of the rare books listed here may only be available at libraries by special request. Most of them can be found in the library of the Scottish Tartans Museum and the Scottish Tartans Society at Fonab House, Pitlochry in Perthshire, Scotland.

**Adam, Frank,** *The Clans, Septs and Regiments of the Scottish Highlands,* W. and A. K. Johnston, Edinburgh, 1908.

**Anderson, William,** *The Scottish Nation,* A. Fullerton, London, 1874.

**Bain, Robert,** *The Clans and Tartans of Scotland,* Collins, London and Glasgow, 1990. Illustrations added 1976.

**Dunbar, John Telfer,** *The Costume of Scotland,* B. T. Batsford, London, 1984.

**Grant, James,** *The Tartans and the Clans of Scotland,* W. A. K. Johnston, Edinburgh, 1886.

**Innes, Thomas,** *Tartans of the Clans and Families of Scotland,* W. and A. K. Johnston, Edinburgh, 1938.

**Logan, James,** *The Scottish Gael or Celtic Manners, as Preserved among the Highlanders,* Smith, Elder & Co., London, 1831.

**Logan, James,** *The Clans of the Scottish Highlands,* illustrated by Robert Ranald Mclan. Ackermann & Co., London, 1845–47.

**MacDonald, Micheil,** *The Clans of Scotland,* Brian Todd, London, 1991.

**MacKay, J. G.,** *The Romantic Story of the Highland Garb and Tartans,* MacKay, Stirling, 1924.

**MacLeod, Rhuairidh,** *Tartans of the Clan McLeod,* MacLeod, Skye, 1990.

**Nesbitt, Robert Chancellor,** *Nesbit of that Ilk,* London, 1941.

**North, C. N. M'Intyre,** *Book of the Club of True Highlanders,* London, 1881.

**Peter, David MacGregor,** *Baronage of Angus and Mearns,* Oliver & Boyd, Edinburgh, 1856.

**Ross, John,** *Land of the Scottish Gael,* The Airlie Press, 1930.

**Smibert, T.,** *The Clans of the Highlands of Scotland,* James Hogg, Edinburgh, 1850.

**Smith, William and Andrew,** *Authenticated Tartans of the Clans and Families of Scotland,* Smith, Mauchline, 1850.

**Stewart, Donald C.,** *The Setts of the Scottish Tartans,* Oliver & Boyd, Edinburgh, 1950. 2nd edition Shepheard-Walwyn, London, 1974.

**Stewart, Donald William,** *Old and Rare Scottish Tartans,* G. P. Johnston, Edinburgh, 1893.

**Stuart, J. S. S.** and **Stuart, C. E.,** *Vestiarium Scoticum,* William Tait, Edinburgh, 1842.

**Teall, Gordon and Smith, Philip,** *District Tartans,* Shepheard-Walwyn Limited, London, 1992.

**Whyte, H.,** *The Scottish Clans and Their Tartans,* W. and A. K. Johnston, Edinburgh, 1891.

**Whyte, H., and others,** *The Tartans of the Clans and Septs of Scotland,* W. and A. K. Johnston, Edinburgh, 1906.

# COLLECTIONS TO VISIT

**U K**

The Carmichael Collection,
the West Highland Museum,
Fort William,
Argyll.

The Cockburn Collection,
the Mitchell Library,
North Street,
Glasgow.

The Highland Society of London Collection,
the Scotttish National Museum,
Queen Street,
Edinburgh.

The Norwich Collection (Bolingbroke & Jones),
the Provost MacBean Collection,
the MacGregor-Hastie Collection,
the J. T. Dunbar Collection (MS Wilson papers),
the Scottish Tartans Museum,
Comrie,
Perthshire.

**U S A**

The Clan Originaux,
Pendleton Mill,
Oregon.

# PICTURE CREDITS